W9-CBM-859

THE UN UNDER ATTACK

The UN Under Attack

Edited by

JEFFREY HARROD
AND
NICO SCHRIJVER

Institute of Social Studies, The Hague
The Netherlands

Gower

Aldershot · Brookfield USA · Hong Kong · Singapore · Sydney

Published by
Gower Publishing Company Limited
Gower House
Croft Road
Aldershot
Hants GU11 3HR
England

Gower Publishing Company
Old Post Road
Brookfield
Vermont 05036
USA

ISBN 0 566 05695 X

Laserset from computer disk by
Ponting–Green Publishing Services
London
Printed in Great Britain by
Athanaeum Press Limited, Newcastle upon Tyne

Contents

JX
1977
.436
1988

Acknowledgements

The editors would like to acknowledge the support and contributions of the following organizations and persons: The Netherlands Association for International Affairs, especially its Chairman, Godfried van Benthem van den Bergh, who organized the lecture series on which the book is based and introduced the speakers; the Institute of Social Studies which provided the forum for the lectures and encouraged the editors to produce this book; Gary Debus of the Institute's Publications Office for his interest, enthusiasm and important work in moving the manuscripts of a lecture series to a publishable final collection. The editors also would like to recognize the efforts of the many production workers at the Institute of Social Studies and Gower for their assistance in producing this book.

Last but not least, the editors would like to thank the various contributors for their patience and prompt and constructive responses to our editorial work in the different stages of the production of this book.

The editors
June 1987

Preface

Sir Shridath Ramphal
Commonwealth Secretary-General

It is both right and necessary that mankind should attempt to bring to relations between nations those norms of democratic governance and equity which have been evolved for the prudent conduct of national affairs. The United Nations and its network of global institutions have, so far, been the highest achievement of this human endeavour. The need for orderly management of relations between nations has grown as their links have become closer and more complex, as their interdependence has increased, and as the consequences of friction between them has become graver. Aspirations to greater equity can also no longer be contained within the bounds of each state; many factors have served to give them a wider reach. Distant deprivation joins neighbourhood need in its claims on our instincts of compassion and justice. The links between poverty for the many and prosperity for the few have also become clearer; so has the danger of their being allowed to co-exist.

But the paradox – and the tragedy – of recent times is that even as the need for better management of relations between nations and for a multilateral approach to global problems has become more manifest, support for internationalism has weakened – eroded by some of the strongest nations whose position behoves them to be at its vanguard and who have in the past acknowledged that obligation of leadership. This is most true, of course, of the United States, whose recent behaviour has served actually to weaken the structures of multilateralism, including the United Nations itself.

These trends spell a drift from partnership and co-operation towards dominance and dictation; they mark a waning of the spirit of internationalism which found expression in the founding of the United Nations system and the gradual strengthening of the structures of multilateral co-operation since then.

The expansion of the World Bank in response to the challenge of third world development; the setting up of the International Development Association (IDA) to extend the Bank's support to the poorest countries; the establishment of the UN Conference on Trade and Development (UNCTAD) as a global forum for advancing North–South co-operation; the addition of Part IV to the General Agreement on Tariffs and Trade (GATT) in recognition of the special needs of developing countries in world trade; the creation of the International Fund for Agricultural Development (IFAD) for a focused approach to averting food deficits: these were among the advances in international co-operation since Bretton Woods and San Francisco. They were possible because of the emergence of a global consensus which responded in some fashion to the consciousness that we were all part of one world community – neighbours needing an ethic of partnership for living together. That enlightened consensus has become a casualty in the drift towards dominance and the ascendancy of unilateralism in world affairs.

Evidence of this drift continues to increase. A few countries chose to deny the Convention on the Law of the Sea the universality of support which years of patient negotiation had brought within reach. The world's most powerful country has turned its back on the World Court, giving rise to questions about its commitment to the rule of law in international relations. Similar questions have been prompted by its failure to honour pledges in respect of contributions to the United Nations, which has placed the world body in unprecedented difficulties. Democratic intervention to secure reforms at the UN Educational, Scientific and Cultural Organization (UNESCO) has been abandoned in favour of unilateral withdrawal. IDA and IFAD, both agencies which help the neediest nations, have suffered as a result of cutbacks in support by the wealthiest nations. Support has been withdrawn from the UN Fund for Population Activities (UNFPA) and the International Planned Parenthood Federation because they refuse to submit their policies to dictation by one country.

The same attitude towards multilateral endeavours has been reflected in the stifling of the North–South dialogue. Discussion of North–South issues has been blocked in global assemblies where democratic principles govern decisions: it is now accommodated only in forums where the dominance of Northern nations is constitutionally assured. And in the councils of such bodies, like the World Bank and the International Monetary Fund (IMF), there has been pressure to make them conform more closely to the ideological fixations of major powers. In the pre-eminence given to market forces, the real needs of development have suffered, and efforts to make financial institutions more effective in meeting global needs have been frustrated.

But, as is so often the case, the ideological fix is an intellectual trap. Countries which have resisted more equitable arrangements for North–South relations base their stand on a distaste for interference with market forces; this also colours the attitude to development aid. But these same countries do not practice at home what they preach abroad. 'Intervention' is widely indulged, sometimes at a basic level of policy, in the national and regional economies of major countries. And it is indulged in support of numerous industries, from farming to steel, shirts to shoes.

Recently there have been moves towards co-ordination of economic policy among leading industrial countries. This is, in principle, better than wholly uncoordinated national action. But co-operation within a directorate of powerful countries is hardly the answer to the world's needs, the needs of all its nations. In fact, it could well have the result of reinforcing the dominance of the few over the many.

No-one can claim perfection for the instruments of global co-operation which exist today. It is in the interest of all nations to work for their reform, for improvement in organizational efficiency and for cost-effectiveness. But such reform must come from processes which respect their global character and the spirit of partnership which is the quintessence of internationalism. It must not be sought through imposition by the strong.

The United Nations is the main instrument we have for resolving the problems facing the world community, preserving civility in the conduct of international relations, and advancing the well-being of all the world's people. The need surely is to strengthen and revitalise the United Nations. It has many accomplishments; but we have yet to exploit its full potential. We may have been spared a world war since the United Nations was set up, but it has hardly been an era of peace. Each day since then, there has been some war, some armed conflict, taking its toll of life in some part of the world. And preparation for bigger wars has gone on unchecked, with the accumulation of weapons of increasingly horrifying power. We have in frenetic fertility multiplied several times over our capacity to destroy the entire world; and militarism has sucked more and more countries into its coils. The obscenity of the nuclear arsenals apart, we now have third world countries committing nearly $250 billion a year to military expenditure – for the greater part with the encouragement and assistance of the richer countries running the 'arms bazaars'. All this is money which could create a better life for people, so many millions of whom are now hungry or malnourished, suffering or dying from preventable illness, without clean water or decent housing: millions of human beings denied human fulfilment, bereft even of hope.

It is through a stronger United Nations, fortified by the collective and enlightened commitment of all its members, that we can strive together to correct these distortions, prevent recourse to arms for the settlement of disputes, and obviate the need for the competitive acquisition of arms. In the United Nations lies our hope for securing progress in peace. To weaken it is to imperil our common future.

The United Nations and its principal agencies can benefit from critical appraisal of their structure and functioning, if such appraisal is informed by a commitment to their central role as instruments of the world community in its efforts to evolve a more secure and more democratic system of world order. I welcome *The UN Under Attack* for its contribution to that assessment.

Introduction

This book originated as a series of public lectures at the Institute of Social Studies at the end of 1985. The lecture series was intended to give recognition to an event and a trend. The event was the 40th anniversary of the United Nations and the trend was the increasing strength of the voices of criticism concerning the performance of the United Nations.

The book appears at a time when the UN's very function as a permanent platform for dialogue and as an agency for international co-operation and operational assistance in the social, cultural and economic sphere is under attack. The United Nations may have grown used to the traditional attacks relating to its collective security function which are usually based on the argument that the collective security provisions have not worked to preserve the peace and that its role in this area has been weak; the current attacks, however, are also directed at the agencies within the UN system, dealing with social, cultural and economic affairs and have reached such a pitch that major States have withdrawn from one of the agencies and are threatening similar action against others. This book, consequently places emphasis on the dangerous erosion of multilateralism in an increasingly interdependent world by a considered review of the social and economic activities and agencies of the United Nations. Each contributor was then asked to address his analysis in the spirit of either a defence, or positive and constructive criticism, of the United Nations and its social and economic agencies.

As a result, the collection represents a compendium of strains of opinion concerning the United Nations, ranging from a defence based purely on the fact that it exists, to one based on the notion that it is one of the most substantive advances in the international history of humanity. Between these ends of the continuum are found detailed accounts and analyses of the history of the current problems, the political reasons for them and substantive recommendations for changes.

It should be noted then that the authors and the contributions are special in two ways which distinguish this collection from others that have appeared in the field of international organization. Firstly, all the authors have served with, or have had experience in dealing with, agencies of the UN system. Many of them speak purely as practitioners of administration and diplomacy within the UN system or the broader international milieu. Others bring a substantive academic perspective to their subject. Despite these latter authors, the collection still departs somewhat from the standard formula of attempting to secure the best-known academic to write about his/her favourite topic. The strength of the collection thus rests to some degree, precisely on the actual experience the authors have had with the UN system.

The second difference is that, with the exception of one author, all the writers have been representatives of, or associated with, The Netherlands. Despite this fact one should not presume any conformity of opinion concerning the UN social and economic activities. However, there can be no doubt that they represent a certain perspective of the international society and the functioning of the UN system that resides in a small, industrially advanced State with a tradition of internationalism and which, despite its economic power, cannot be counted among the major powers. This may be important at this juncture when all too often the dominant voices of protest come not only from the larger States but even from non-governmental organizations and political parties of such States.

The finished collection brings together ten contributions, most of which are derived from the lectures as presented in the lecture series. Four of them deal with some general aspects of the UN system, changes in the political and negotiating environment concerning collective security, developments in decision making, the UN role in the development of international law and the possibility of the existing United Nations serving as a basis for the creation of a more powerful world authority.

Two chapters cover the UN-associated agencies dealing with economic issues – the International Monetary Fund (IMF), the World Bank, the UN Conference on Trade and Development (UNCTAD) and the General Agreement on Tariffs and Trade (GATT). The remaining four chapters consider the specialized agencies dealing with cultural and socio-economic issues. The International Labour Organization (ILO) and the UN Educational, Scientific and Cultural Organization (UNESCO) are dealt with specifically while other agencies, such as the Food and Agriculture Organization (FAO) and the World Health Organization (WHO) are considered through the perspective of world food security and the theoretical and political aspects of the agencies' recent history.

The editors do hope, as Sir Shridath Ramphal noted in his preface, that this collection and others like it will contribute to a more informed opinion and critique of the United Nations in general and its social, cultural and economic activities in particular.

Jeffrey Harrod
Nico Schrijver
The Hague, 1987

1 Transformations within the United Nations

Hugo Scheltema*

Before discussing some selected transformations within the United Nations I would like to revert to the general title of this collection produced to celebrate the 40th year of existence of the United Nations, namely, *The UN Under Attack*. This heading certainly reflects today's reality but it should not be forgotten that the United Nations has been under attack throughout the whole of its 40-year history. I vividly remember, for example, when I first served in New York 30 years ago, banners in the street carrying the words 'Get the UN out of the US and the US out of the UN'. These words have not, even today, become obsolete. There are still those who do not believe in, or are opposed to, the idea of a universal organization. This sentiment is mainly, but not exclusively, found in the United States. The current terminology used to attack the United Nations is not unlike that which was used at the very beginning of the organization. Inasmuch as the words of attack have changed they have changed because the organization has changed. It is important then to look at some of these changes, or transformations, as they have occurred over the past 40 years.

Over time all organizations evolve but in the case of the United Nations I prefer the notion of 'transformation' rather than 'evolution' because some of the transformations which have taken place are so radical that they may even seem to

* *Hugo Scheltema* is a former ambassador of The Netherlands and is currently Vice-Chairman of The Netherlands Association for International Affairs. Between 1951 and 1955 he was a member of the Dutch permanent mission to the United Nations in New York and from 1978 to 1983 he was Permanent Representative of The Netherlands to the United Nations. In that capacity he was President of the Economic and Social Council in 1979 and Chairman of the UNICEF Board in 1982–83. In 1983 he represented The Netherlands on the Security Council.

lack a constitutional basis in the Charter. The following transformations and symbolic examples of them are selected from many which could be discussed but I have placed some emphasis on the developments within the collective security and diplomatic areas of the UN work as this has been the area of my most active participation.

Four transformations will be briefly discussed:

1. the quantitative transformation: from UN family to UN system,
2. the transformation of practices and procedures of the Security Council: from public debate to private consensus,
3. the transformation of the operations of the Security Council: from collective security to peace-keeping,
4. the transformation of attitudes towards issues on the international agenda: from national sovereignty to international discussion.

The Quantitative Transformation

The quantitative transformation is obvious and well-known but nevertheless needs to be constantly stressed because it affects so many other aspects of transformation. What was originally an organization of those states that emerged victoriously from the Second World War has grown into a world-wide system with near universal membership. The growth from 51 member States to 159 member States has been a transformation from what used to be called a UN family of a select few states (although in historical perspective still a universal group) to a system comprised of more sub-divisions and agencies than was ever foreseen in 1945. There are now 16 specialized agencies and numerous other bodies and institutions dealing with public affairs on a global level because they can no longer be dealt with effectively at the national level. In the late 1940s when the new UN building was being designed the best guess at future membership was 90 member States at the maximum. This latter guess was symbolic of the inability in the early days to foresee the developments we are considering today after 40 years. It is also symbolic of the reasons why some transformations have taken place outside the formal structure.

Transformation of the Practices and Procedures of the Security Council

As is well known the Security Council was conceived in 1945 as the supreme body for the purpose of presiding over peace and security. It was conceived, however, from the perspective of those who had won the Second World War and within the general philosophy that those who had emerged victoriously in war would remain and rule victoriously in peace. This illusion was embodied in the Charter and it soon became clear that it was indeed an illusion because the five powers to whom this particular universal task was entrusted quickly disagreed on their main international duty. From this point of view, then, the Charter became obsolete.

There were other Charter provisions that became obsolete almost from the beginning. The idea of an international police power under the United Nations that could act under Chapter VII of the Charter in case of conflict, is one example. The concept of a Military Staff Committee is another. It is curious but important to note that this latter Committee still meets once a month with two items on the agenda – the date of the next meeting and the menu for the next meeting. That the Committee continues to meet, however, is one indication of the way changes have taken place without formally violating or changing the Charter but without at the same time following its literal meaning.

Such was the case with the change in practices and procedures in the Security Council. In the early days the Security Council was the world's top forum for public debate, for recrimination and victory, and for veto and double veto. Intimate knowledge of the rules of procedure and skill to handle them in open and unprepared exchanges were the basic requirements for representatives of the Council. The transformation which took place started in the late 1960s when private and informal consultations began to precede the actual sessions of the Council.

This development had a physical manifestation. During the 1970s a special consultation chamber was built adjacent to the actual Council Chamber. It is an exact replica of the Council Chamber itself but on a much smaller scale. It is accessible only to members of the Council and not to representatives of other missions, media or public. Matters brought before the Council are first discussed in lobbies or in the President's office, and subsequently in the Consultation Room where the fifteen members meet in relative informality and in complete seclusion. Here it should be noted, that the non-aligned members of the council had sought and obtained the right to make use of the Consultation Room to the exclusion of the non non-aligned. Thus in 1983 the five permanent members and two aligned non-permanent members, Poland and The Netherlands were excluded. This is a clear indication of the changed balance of power.

Thus decisions of the Council are 'precooked' and are ready for public presentation when the Council finally meets in open and formal session. As the door opens and non-member missions, media and a sprinkling of the public are waiting, the fifteen members of the Council file in like a court of justice, ready to render their verdict.

The members of the Council thus enter the public session knowing precisely what they have done, knowing precisely what decisions have been taken and knowing precisely what the procedures at the Council meeting will be, including the occasional veto. In addition, members of the Council each read their written statements, which are prepared in advance, and then non-members are allowed to make statements. Because so many non-members are admitted it is sometimes said that the Security Council has transformed itself into a mini-General Assembly.

What has really happened is that the Security Council has transformed itself from a forum for public debate and veto into a deliberative body seeking consensus behind closed doors. Public sessions have lost their relevance and the Council now functions as a different instrument. But it must be recognized that the Council still functions, it functions now as a permanent instrument of persuasion and consensus with its main characteristic being its constant availability.

Transformation of the Operations of the Security Council

Perhaps a more obvious transformation, or rather innovation, has been the development of peace-keeping. No discourse on the 40 years of the United Nations could be complete without the peace-keeping operations as one of the main features.

Peace-keeping was invented by creative political minds during the Suez crisis in 1956 and has since been practised in the Congo, the Middle East, Cyprus and elsewhere under varying mandates. The essence of peace-keeping is that it is not peace-making. There is no coercion and no enforcement action under Chapter VII of the Charter. Any peace-keeping operation is based on the consensus of all parties concerned. This may be its weakness but at the same time it ensures a certain level of effectiveness as it is a physical expression of a collective determination to manage a crisis.

Peace-keeping is an innovation, a transformation of the operations of the Security Council which I consider to be a proof of universal creative thinking. Its success is hard to prove and, although it may not sound convincing, it is certain that situations would have been a lot worse without UN peace-keeping. Peace-keeping operations have now secured a permanent place in the complex of UN activities. The interesting point here is that UN peace-keeping, as developed over the past 30 years, has no explicit constitutional basis but equally nothing in the Charter prevents its use.

Transformation of Attitudes Towards International Issues

Over the past 40 years one of the great impetuses to transformation has been the expansion of particular issues of international concern which have crept into the reality of the world. There are many areas and issues which are now openly discussed and considered legitimate for discussion that 40 years ago, would have been considered as clear and unacceptable intervention in the domestic affairs of member States. The general subject of human rights is a most striking example of this new international thinking and practice.

4

Do such transformations which have taken place represent a crisis of the UN system and the basis for attacks upon it? In answer to this question I would like to point to two interconnected factors which must be considered: first, that so-called crises tend to be crises at the fringe of the system and not at its heart; and second, upon which the first is founded, that the essence of the UN system can be seen as its quality of 'availability'.

Crisis at the Fringe

Much of the talk of crisis concerns the so-called non-political activities of the United Nations found in the various bodies and agencies dealing with economic and social matters.

There has been much growth of activity in the non-political areas. The reason for this is tied up with action by the United Nations. One of the most noticeable developments of the past 40 years has been the completion of the process of decolonialization that has taken place in and through the United Nations and it is precisely this process which created the new world unforeseen in 1945. It is clear that the United Nations reacted quickly as a collective institution to supply the machinery and be available to take the place of a system which was no longer in existence. This growth of social and economic activity has yielded new institutions and new machinery – for example, for the first time in history there exist bodies which deal with obvious universal problems such as refugees, environment or atomic energy.

Many of these organizations and agencies have been attacked in the past and most of them have survived. The International Labour Organization (ILO) is a case in point. The large bodies operating in the social and economic field, as the World Bank, the International Monetary Fund (IMF) and the UN Food and Agriculture Organization (FAO) all operate on a universal basis and show elements of vitality.

Currently there is a crisis in the UN Educational, Scientific and Cultural Organization (UNESCO). But this crisis and others similar to it are not, I submit, crises of the heart of the UN system, they are crises at the fringe. At its 40th anniversary the characteristic of the United Nations is vitality, not imminent collapse. This becomes even more evident when one considers my main point – that of the constant availability of the UN diplomatic machinery.

The Availability of the UN Diplomatic Machinery

If I may be permitted one more symbolic example of the role of the United Nations in today's diplomacy I would like to mention the change within continuity which has occurred at the New York UN gatherings of heads of state and diplomats.

In 1951 and earlier the heads of state who came to the opening sessions of the General Assembly were very visible. They used to talk to each other, they used to be in restaurants and, in effect, be open to the public. Today, as when I was there recently, they are protected by helicopters, and First Avenue is no longer accessible to the population of New York city.

The interesting point is that despite this tremendous change in style the heads of state still, after 40 years, continue to go to such events as the opening of the General Assembly or even the celebration of the 40th year of the United Nations. One of the ideas at the beginning, and spelled out in the Charter, was that the United Nations should be an international forum and it is clear that it still functions effectively as such. Over one hundred prominent statesmen, including heads of state from all over the world converge on First Avenue. Would they do so if they considered the organization to be irrelevant? The United Nations continues to be the obvious annual meeting place. It is the world's biggest diplomatic supermarket.

The basic reason for such continued support is the constant availability of the UN machinery. Instruments provided by the United Nations are permanently there, whether it be for mother and child care, human rights, technical and monetary assistance or peace and security. Some of these instruments need not be used on a daily basis but their value is simply in 'being there'. In matters of peace and security there is available a world machinery of a size and with an experience that has never existed before in history. If nations in conflict or near conflict are willing to make use of that machinery it is there. The Security Council is a source of permanent possibilities for dealing with international problems – through the Secretary General, through mediation or personal intervention or through a specially constructed, if limited, body. If all these instruments supplied to the world do not work well, then it is the world which is to blame, not the organization.

Conclusion

At the beginning I mentioned the obsolete nature of many parts of the UN Charter. I have indicated some ways in which transformations and changes have been made and concluded that the crises which exist are at the fringe of the system and that the availability of the UN machinery is a basic aspect which helps retain its relevance.

Although the original conception of the Charter may be obsolete the Charter itself has not stood in the way of such transformation, innovation or growth which were not foreseen by the founding fathers. If, in a sense, the Charter has become obsolete, beware of tampering with it for it contains some high explosives. Fortunately there has never been any serious effort to review it and creative activities, such as peace-keeping, have been successful even without a firm constitutional base. In other words, and in conclusion, the merit of the United

Nations is to have grown to full maturity despite its Charter and it has been able to do so because of the flexibility, inventiveness and creative spirit of those who deal with the organization.

2 The United Nations as a World Authority

Silviu Brucan*

Most of the chapters in this book are devoted to the past 40 years of the United Nations. I propose to focus on its future. After all, it is the future of the United Nations rather than its past that we can do something about.

My general premise is that the international conditions that produced the United Nations at the middle of this century have changed so much that what we need now, at the end of the century, is a different type of international institution capable of coping with the new world problems that have arisen in the meantime.

Hence, I advocate the transformation of the United Nations, which is based essentially on the political will of 160 sovereign states, into a world institution holding power and political will of its own and having the authority and competence to plan, make decisions, and enforce them. The point is that the threat of nuclear war is too serious for world affairs to be determined by individual nation–states or by the ambitious aims of the superpowers.

The Case for a World Authority

In this section, the historical and political case for a World Authority is made.

* *Silviu Brucan* is Professor of Political Science at the University of Bucharest. He has been the Romanian Ambassador in Washington, D.C. and Permanent Representative to the United Nations in New York. He was editor of Romania's largest circulation newspaper and also head of the Romanian broadcasting system. He has written extensively on many aspects of international relations.

It should be remembered that 40 years ago the founders of the United Nations proceeded from the classic theories of international law elaborated at a time when European states functioned as self-contained social systems whose decisions originated chiefly from within. Thus, they drafted the UN Charter as a constitution for a model of the world in which the main actor and almighty decision-maker was the nation–state functioning on the basis of national sovereignty. Of course, power being above the law, the Big Five of the victorious coalition in World War II reserved for themselves a privileged position as permanent members of the Security Council with the right to veto Council decisions that do not suit them. The whole arrangement reflected the ideology of an epoch in which power realities were skilfully disguised in the liberal rhetoric of international law.

The practical consequence has been that the United Nations is unable to take effective action whenever one of the great powers is directly or indirectly involved in a conflict. Thus since the great powers are omnipresent on the world stage, very few military outbreaks can be resolved by the United Nations. Moreover, the principle of national sovereignty dominating the United Nations allows member States to disregard decisions that do not please them. The United Nations could do nothing to stop South Africa from invading territories of neighboring countries, or Israel from bombing targets in distant states and is impotent in dealing with such an absurd war as that between Iraq and Iran. As for the General Assembly, any draft resolution must be watered down in order to gain the support of a majority of member States. As a result, the number of votes in favour of a resolution grows in inverse proportion to the substance of its recommendations. One can safely predict that a resolution enjoying an unanimous vote will have no practical consequence whatsoever.

Perhaps the most disappointing performance of the United Nations has been on the issue of the insane nuclear arms race which threatens the very existence of humankind. Initially, disarmament negotiations were supposed to bring about reductions in weaponry. Today, that logic has been reversed: it is the building of new weapon systems that requires arms talks. Churchill's famous watchword 'Arm to Parley' should now be 'Parley to Arm'.

Indeed, during twenty years or so of UN Disarmament Committee meetings, the cost of arms production and military expenditure has risen from $200 billion per annum to almost $1 trillion. In the process, the very notion of disarmament has been shown to be irrelevant since not one single machine-gun has been scrapped as a result of such negotiations. Arms control is a notion much more appropriate to present-day power politics as it allows for agreements about rules and limits within which the parties could further engage in the arms race. The key-word of SALT I and SALT II is *limitation*. But under the aegis of these agreements the number of the most horrifying weapons of mass destruction has multiplied. The whole exercise has produced a new diplomatic profession, namely arms negotiators, which offers the possibility for a distinguished career and a much more enduring and rewarding one than traditional diplomacy. In fact, arms negotiation may provide lifetime employment. Among insiders at Geneva, a favourite joke goes like this: when a diplomat is sent on a mission, he books a hotel room: when he is appointed to an embassy post, he rents an apartment. But when he is selected for arms talks in Geneva, he buys a house.

Even though the superpowers have acquired the capability to destroy each other many times over, the arms race continues. In order to justify the resulting increase in military expenditure to the taxpayer, who is required to accept painful cuts in social welfare and make other sacrifices, governments must show they are engaged in serious arms negotiations with the intention of reducing military expenditure. In other words, without arms talks the sky-rocketing military expenditures would not be possible. In short, disarmament negotiations have become the *public relations facet of the arms race*. Modern weapons, like any other product, could not be sold without the Geneva-based advertising campaign. The battle in the US Congress over the MX missile is a striking illustration of that marketing technique. During the debate, nobody seriously argued about the military value of the MX and rightly so. Originally, the MX was meant to be a mobile missile that would offset the vulnerability of the US land-based missiles with an inter-continental range (ICBMs). But since this proved not possible, the Reagan administration decided to base the MX in existing missile silos, making them perfect stationary targets. Hence, the only argument left was to present the MX as a bargaining chip in the Geneva talks with the USSR. Congressmen were warned that a vote against it would undermine the United States' negotiating position. To make the case more persuasive, the chief US negotiator in Geneva was brought to Washington to argue that modern weapons are now produced for the sake of negotiations rather than for the battlefield. Although the vote was very close, the bill went through Congress and the winner was: MX Kampelman.

I will conclude this discussion of the United Nations' record in matters of peace, international security and disarmament by noting that the United Nations cannot be blamed for all that is happening in the world today. Let me state clearly that I dissociate myself from the critics of the United Nations who deny the positive role it plays in promoting important and worthy causes in our troubled world. I am equally opposed to those who want to see the United Nations abolished, like the rightist Heritage Foundation in Washington, which views the United Nations as an obstacle to imperial policies.

We should pay tribute to the United Nations' tremendous contribution to the decolonization process and the formation of numerous new, independent States. While decolonization is primarily the result of the fierce struggle waged by peoples under the colonial yoke, the United Nations has been instrumental in facilitating and legalizing the formation of new states and promoting their international recognition. Thus, the United Nations has contributed to the extension of the state system to Africa, Asia and Latin America, eventually making the state system virtually universal.

More specifically, some specialized UN agencies carry out useful activities: for example, the lives of some four hundred thousand youngsters under the age of five are saved every year by the UN International Children's Emergency Fund (UNICEF). The UN Development Programme (UNDP) spends $675 to $700 million each year in subsidizing projects with long-term consequences in the poorest countries of the world. The UN High Commissioner for Refugees (UNHCR) must also be mentioned for saving tens of thousands of people, providing them with shelter, food and an acceptable environment in various parts of the world. A remarkable job in fighting illiteracy and spreading education in developing countries is performed by the UN Educational, Scientific and Cultural Organization (UNESCO). Finally, the rapidly-executed and effective campaign initiated by the United Nations to help millions of Africans struck by drought and famine was very impressive.

Although such humanitarian activities may well continue, the United Nations was, nevertheless, neither conceived, structured nor developed to deal with the critical global problems threatening the very existence of humankind at the end of this century.

The Current Global Problems

The world of the next decades will be a 'small world' in which the per capita GNP of the developed nations will still be twelve times that of the developing nations, even if the growth rates set by the United Nations for the year 2000 were to be achieved. The population of the developing nations, however, will be five times that of the developed world. Anyone who puts these two sets of figures together must realize that the explosion will not be able to be limited to population. We will live in a world in which it will take two to three hours to fly from Caracas to New York, or from Lagos to London, a world in which the Bolivian, the Pakistani and the Lebanese will see on television how people live in an affluent society, a world in which there will be no suburbia where the rich may insulate themselves from the poor.

As the insane nuclear race is being extended into outer space, the world of the next decades will live and perhaps sleep with the balance-of-terror in the hands of 20 or so ambitious nations armed with atomic weapons, not to mention terrorist groups using atomic weapons for blackmail or ransom. As the pillars of the old order crumble one after the other, the world will look like New York, Tokyo or Paris without traffic regulations or policemen.

Could all these trends be arrested and world order maintained by the kind of international institution we now have? Surely, to deal with such global problems a decision-making system with 160 independent participants having conflicting interests, objectives and views is in itself a prescription for ineffectiveness. In a world divided by so many discrepancies in power, wealth and ideology, each member State will fight fiercely to promote its own self-interest on any issue of security, trade, or development. The principle of national sovereignty enshrined in the Charter is a clear invitation to do so.

But what is national sovereignty in a nuclear war? Could any state, however large or small, stop nuclear rockets at its borders? The very notion of national security has lost its meaning in the nuclear era. We are all in the same boat.

As for economics and finance, recent fluctuations on the world money and commodity markets make it abundantly clear that we are dealing with a global economic crisis the effects of which are largely beyond the control of national governments, whether in the West or the East. Not even the greatest world economic power, the United States, can eliminate its alarming budgetary deficit while goods produced by the United States are losing ground in world markets. Because of world economic conditions the greatest financial power is also becoming the greatest debtor nation in absolute terms. In Eastern Europe, there was a time when we thought that our central planning system made the socialist economy immune to disturbances in the world market. We are discovering the hard way that this is not so. Briefly, economic crisis, like nuclear war, is global; it affects everybody and no single nation or group of nations alone can overcome it. Only global solutions will suffice.

And yet, the United Nations is not equipped to deal with global problems, let alone to promote global solutions. At the time of Bretton Woods or the Havana conferences, from which the World Bank, the International Monetary Fund (IMF) and indirectly the General Agreement on Tariffs and Trade (GATT) ensued, the initiators of such organizations were the rich industrial nations of the West. Quite naturally, they created the institutions which they themselves required to regulate international trade and finances according to their specific interests. The Gold Exchange Standard institutionalized the supremacy of the US dollar; the World Bank and IMF have displayed a special preference for the stimulus of Western private capital in third world countries. Although the developing nations made strenuous efforts to secure the transfer of capital from the rich nations through special UN funds for economic development and thus avoid being left at the mercy of Western donors, capital transfers have remained mostly under the control of the latter. The fact is that at the time when all these international agencies and banks were created, the third world, as we understand it today, simply did not exist and hence its interests were not taken into account.

It was only in the early seventies that the third world succeeded in rallying its forces and saw to it that at the 1974 Special Session of the General Assembly an historic resolution was adopted on the establishment of a New International Economic Order. The UN Conference on Trade and Development (UNCTAD) was created as a response to GATT's policies, and the World Bank was to move a little in support of development strategies though the industrial nations are still in a position to decide how the Bank's funds are to be used. Lately, the Reagan administration has been exerting heavy pressure upon developing nations to denationalize industries and deregulate the public sector in order to open the door to multinational corporations.

Currently, however, rocketing foreign debts and a sharp decline in raw material prices are severely undermining third world economies. The result is that developing nations can neither pay their debt nor import industrial products thus threatening both the international financial system and Western exports. On the other hand, the OECD countries are already saturated with industrial products and even the biggest trading nation of the West, the United States, is unable to balance its foreign trade by increasing its exports despite the 30 per cent decline of the dollar that was expected to make American goods more competitive on world markets. In the meantime, three vast continents, plus the socialist nations, eagerly await the industrial equipment from the West.

Clearly, only global planning and management can overcome such a contradictory economic situation in which all parties suffer. But as things stand now, the United Nations is unable to perform such a task for the very simple reason that it was based on the assumption that national economic decisions are chiefly determined by domestic conditions.

The fact is that forces and trends within the world economy impinge more and more upon decisions made by national governments. I suggest that we are now going through a transitory period in the history of international relations – from the interstate system to the emerging world system. Whereas in the former the input from the nation–states is predominant and decisive in shaping the system and determining its behaviour, in the latter the process is reversed, that is, the world system is beginning to prevail over its subsystems, adjusting all of them to its global motion.

It is against this theoretical background that I advocate the creation of a world institution which should reconcile elements of the inter-state system still in force with those of the coming world system.

Research and Action Towards a World Authority

International and transnational activities are becoming so interdependent and systematic that the world system is acquiring a driving force of its own which transcends nation–states. But since this driving force has no conscious direction nor rationality, it is imperative that a World Authority be established to perform this role.

Such a World Authority, however, is merely an abstract idea. To bring it down to earth a serious intellectual effort is required. Here are my suggestions regarding the main directions of such research work and how to proceed.

1. The first question involves the management of power in international society, namely ways and means must be worked out to establish an international institution wielding power of its own. In practical terms, this means that a transfer of power (a partial and gradual one, of course) from the nation–states to the new institutions would have to take place. The

13

transfer of power to the World Authority being assumed to be gradual, it follows that during the transitory period world order will be kept by a duality of power: the nation–state retaining most of its sovereign rights and the World Authority exercising power in international affairs to the extent of its delegated authority and competence.

2. The concept of World Authority is different from that of world government. The latter presupposes the dissolution of states and their replacement by a single governing body designed to run the whole world. The World Authority requires the nation–states to be retained with only a partial transfer of power to the new institution so as to enable it to operate effectively within its limited area of competence.

3. The assumption is that the World Authority will be initially entrusted with two major tasks: *peace maintenance* and the *restructuring of international economic relations*. Securing peace means restructuring the current system of international relations, more particularly, bringing to a halt the arms race, the momentum of which should be reversed thus leading to complete disarmament and eventually the elimination of war. This also involves the establishment of a *World Tribunal* to make sure that the decisions of the World Authority are enforced and a *World Police Force* to intervene whenever international law is violated and to settle disputes peacefully.

4. The choice of the form of government of the national economic, social and political system will remain the inalienable right of each nation. The World Authority will see to it that no foreign power interferes with such internal affairs of member States. It is only the *use of force* in interstate relations that will fall within the competence of the World Authority.

5. While nations are extremely sensitive about their sovereign rights, experience shows that they are nevertheless prepared to transfer some of their sovereignty provided the advantages outweigh any disadvantages. For example, recognizing that it is in their best interest to allow foreign civilian airplanes to fly over their territories, national governments have accepted the establishment of the International Civil Aviation Organization (ICAO) and have abided strictly by its rules. Also, such activities as weather control, shipping and the control of contagious diseases have been entrusted to international institutions wielding power of their own. Therefore, a thorough study should be undertaken of the possibility of extending such institutions to more sensitive issues like peace and security.

6. Confidence-building measures are essential in the case of a supranational institution, particularly on issues where fear and suspicion are rife.

7. Economics of a warless world: the question of conversion to a peace economy must be re-examined in the context of the present economic crisis and of a strategy for development.

8. Politics of a warless world: what kind of restrictions and pressures should be applied to prevent states, particularly great powers, from using force?

9. Law of a warless world: a totally new legal framework must be formulated keeping in mind the conceptual novelty of a supranational institution. The new Charter must spell out clearly what kind of safeguards will be necessary to prevent organs of the new institution from encroaching upon areas remaining under the authority of nation–states.

10. The new institution, namely the World Authority and its enforcement agencies, must be conceived and set up by function, in terms of membership, structure, organizations, distribution of power and representation, policy-making and executive bodies, secretariat, rules of procedure, etc. Here, the authors will have to design the new institution in such a way as to allay the fears that the World Authority, once constituted, may abuse its powers and become a Frankenstein monster which will terrorize nations. This issue is paramount in terms of political feasibility; for unless we assure people that they need not fear abuses perpetrated by the World Authority, the political will for establishing the new institution is not likely to be forthcoming. Equally important is to convey the feeling that there will be fair and equal opportunities for all nations, irrespective of size, power and wealth.

In practical terms, the United Nations could be instrumental in the initiation of the new world body providing the proper forum for discussion of the principles, organization and structure of this new institution, and its experienced staff and vast facilities.

Conclusions

I am perfectly aware that the World Authority is a highly utopian scheme in our world. But since under *realpolitik* the nuclear arms race is regarded as a natural phenomenon, as something inherent in the inter-state system, I would rather be utopian than realist.

It should be remembered that all projections into the future have been considered utopian for the very simple reason that people are thinking about the future in terms of present-day realities and the natural temptation is to think that the future would look like the present, only more so. The classic illustration of this is mediaeval man who used to view the future world as one having more churches, more cathedrals, more castles and more tournaments with brave knights fighting on horseback.

Today the modern world is changing before our eyes and because we refuse to see the changes and thus forego the possibility of adapting to them, the situation is getting more chaotic and unmanageable. On the international scene, changes occur so rapidly that political thought and institutions trail badly behind such changes. In no other field is there so great a contrast between the speed of change and the political institutions supposed to deal with changes. We lack an international institution to deal with the horrendous problems piling up which threaten our jobs, the peace we cherish, the cities we live in, and in the last analysis, our very existence as human beings.

In a world divided by power, wealth and ideology, probably the most difficult assignment is to build a model for the World Authority equally attractive and reassuring for all nations. Paradoxically, those who need it most fear it most, and, therefore, a World Authority, however rational and urgent the forces calling for its establishment are, and however persuasive the historical case for its foundation, the very idea of such an Authority is bound to encounter formidable resistance.

Perhaps the greatest merit of this idea is to make people think about it.

3 Developments in Decision Making in the United Nations

Johan Kaufmann*

Historical Background

For better understanding of the current situation it is indispensable to return to the events and thoughts surrounding the establishment of the United Nations. Both in the political and in the economic area the founders of the United Nations were anxious to avoid repetition of what happened in the period between the two World Wars.[1] In the political sphere, the system laid down in the UN Charter was based on the assumption of a unity concerning ends (and presumably also means) among the five permanent members of the Security Council. East–West rivalry, starting as early as the Yalta Conference and continuing into the Cold War has played havoc with this idealistic set-up. While in the opinion of most observers even the present functioning of the United Nations in dispute settlement is distinctly superior to that of the League of Nations, there can also be no doubt that the hopes of the founders that the Security Council would deal

* *Johan Kaufmann* is a former ambassador of The Netherlands and is currently a member of various official advisory bodies in the field of international relations. Between 1961 and 1969 he was Permanent Representative of The Netherlands to the United Nations and other intergovernmental organizations in Geneva and from 1974 to 1978 Permanent Representative to the United Nations in New York. Upon his retirement he was Professor Extraordinary at the University of Leyden. He has published on international relations, conference diplomacy and UN decision making.

rapidly and efficiently with most, if not all, international conflicts have not been fulfilled.

In the economic sphere, the UN Charter was perhaps equally as innovative as in the part dealing with peace-keeping. The errors of the years of the Great Depression, such as protectionist 'begger-thy-neighbour' policies, which had led to much misery and unemployment, were to be avoided by a new system that could be described as one of collective economic security, somewhat parallel to that of collective political security. It is remarkable that agreement was reached, given the fact that there were important differences of views between the Americans, the British, and the Russians. In the negotiation for the creation of the Bretton Woods Organizations (IMF, IBRD) it had become apparent that the United States wanted to have a set of clear rules which would more or less automatically provide for an orderly international financial system. The British, under the impact of their great wartime physical losses, aimed at a system that would tend to provide financial assistance beyond that which would seem to follow from automatic rules. Keynes, the main negotiator for the British, wanted to insert in the rules of the International Monetary Fund (IMF) a proviso that would ensure action by creditor nations. He had in mind, of course, the United States and the prospect – which was the strong belief of many at that time – of a permanent dollar storage. At the same time, the British did not want a system that meant too much interference with autonomy in economic decisions, specifically the presumed need to maintain discriminatory trade arrangements, such as the imperial preference system, over an extended period of time. Keynes' proposal for action in the field of commodities (an essential part of the still-born International Trade Organization) fitted into this approach, and anticipated the later problems of developing countries.

The idea of a central economic role for the United Nations (Chapters IX and X of the Charter) had not fallen from the sky. The United States had proposed at the Dumbarton Oaks conference a small co-ordinating body for economic and social matters to be subordinate to the General Assembly. The British and Russians did not like this proposal. The British, interestingly, believed that economic and social matters should come generally under the Security Council;[2] they were against bringing economic and social problems under the general United Nations. At San Francisco the small states obtained the upgrading of the Economic and Social Council (ECOSOC) to a 'principal organ of the United Nations'. Chapters IX and X on International Economic and Social Co-operation and the ECOSOC make impressive reading, even today. The all-embracing language of Article 55 concerning, *inter alia*, the promotion of economic and social development together with the right of initiative for ECOSOC in Article 62 made it possible to engage in important work. Indeed, in the early years that is precisely what ECOSOC did, for example, by initiating the early studies on national and international measures for full employment, measures for international economic stability, and measures for the economic development of underdeveloped countries. These were ground-breaking initiatives and were imbued by a spirit of genuine international co-operation.

The Charter assumes that a 'conference approach' to international economic matters could be combined with a negotiating formula. The key phrase in this connection is Article 56 of the Charter: 'All Members pledge themselves to take *joint* and separate action in co-operation with the Organization for the achievement of the purposes set forth in article 55' (author's emphasis). Joint action is, of course, not conceivable without negotiations within a conference framework. In the course of the years, debate and negotiation became increasingly entangled in a manner which was unconstructive. The assumption of the Charter has, however, been fulfilled to a degree which the optimists will surely qualify as 'considerable' and the pessimists see as 'disappointing'.

Old and New Actors within the UN System

The system laid down in the Charter was also based on the assumption that only governments participate in decision-making at the United Nations. Moreover, according to the rules of the General Assembly which are based on the Charter, governments were presumed to be voting and acting individually. An exception to this overwhelming role of governments was the right of initiative given to the Secretary-General, under Article 99 of the Charter, to bring any matter threatening international peace or security to the attention of the Security Council. It soon became apparent that actors additional to individual governments were to make their appearance: firstly, governments started to function as groups which conceivably could be seen as a part-way step towards the joint action by all member States prescribed in Article 56 of the UN Charter. The continuance of the Cold War and the formation of North Atlantic Treaty Organization (NATO) and the Warsaw Pact intensified the early habit of bloc voting, based on group positions of NATO and Warsaw Pact countries respectively. The United States and its allies, being numerically superior, regularly outvoted the USSR and its allies. The automatic majority was not considered as any kind of tyranny by those in the majority. Group positions were officially sanctioned for electoral matters, as, for example, the election of the president and the vice-presidents of the General Assembly. For many important matters *ad hoc* coalitions were formed. This was typically the case for certain economic matters. Thus the establishment of the UN Special Fund in 1958 was possible, the scope of which was determined by a more manageable problem ('pre-investment') than the ambitious set-up of Special United Nations Fund for Economic Development (SUNFED) because a group of like-minded countries, including Brazil, India, Yugoslavia, Denmark and The Netherlands was able to negotiate a compromise between extremists on both sides, that is, the United States which (wishing to eliminate competition with the World Bank and the IMF from an institution like the United Nations where the United States did not control the votes) rejected the idea of any organization bearing a resemblance to SUNFED and certain developing countries which insisted on the need for a full-fledged Capital Development Fund.[3] The early existence of the phenomenon of group acting in UN decision making should be remembered because the impression is sometimes created that this is something new since the formation in 1964 of the Group of 77 developing countries and of the Non-Aligned Movement.

Another unforeseen development was that the secretariat (or rather specific parts of the secretariat) started to play a role in decision making (separate from the powers given the Secretary-General in the UN Charter). Especially in the economic sector the UN secretariat became active in promoting certain ideas, sometimes by peddling fully elaborated draft resolutions among state delegations. Some of these delegations were eager to co-operate with the secretariat, for a variety of reasons, in order, for example, to secure secretariat backing for their own initiatives. To the degree that the secretariat, especially in the early years, was the originator of needed international activity, this practice is quite acceptable. If, however, it leads to biased origins of decision making, contrary to the consensus principle, it cannot be considered as positive.

Similarly, chairmen have assumed tasks beyond the formal powers foreseen in the General Assembly rules of procedure. It has become normal practice that a presiding officer mediates in a conflict situation. In the Security Council such a role of the President is of course considered normal.[4] Another group of new actors was soon constituted by the Non-Governmental Organizations. In accordance with the ground-breaking Article 71 of the UN Charter on arrangements for consultation with Non-Governmental Organizations (NGOs), the ECOSOC formally recognized NGOs from an early date and gave them status in terms of the right to submit or receive papers, the right to make written or oral statements, etc. In the General Assembly no similar arrangements exist, at least not formally. Yet, especially in the field of human rights, NGOs were active from an early date, and often played a far from negligible role in decision making and in negotiations, particularly by preparing draft resolutions. There is little doubt that the role and involvement of the private sector will gradually increase. It is desirable that in each important UN undertaking the provisions made for the participation of NGOs should be examined to see if improvements could be made. Indeed the United Nations Charter was based on the co-operation of the peoples of the United Nations. However, as Alger[5] has pointed out, many of the 4615 international NGOs have limited influence because they do not have strong grassroots participation in their activities, their policies being made by a small elite in their national headquarters. In some cases specialized agencies and other UN bodies have considered certain NGOs which have voiced constant criticisms, as an 'irritant'.

The private sector has gradually assumed a variety of modes of participation in the UN decision-making process. In many specific negotiations the private sector actively participates, as in the case of the cocoa negotiations under the auspices of UNCTAD. In the case of the Commission on Transnational Corporations, representatives of the private sector are formally incorporated; representatives of the trade unions and universities are appointed as expert advisers, who individually or as a group may be consulted by the executive director of the UN Centre on Transnational Corporations or by the Commission itself.[6]

The above remarks were based essentially on the United Nations but in the broader UN system various specialized agencies have different modes of decision making. In the World Bank and the IMF the size of participation in the share capital determines the weight of each participant's vote. In the International Labour Organization (ILO) the long-established tripartite system admits employers and trade unionists as full participants in decision making.

In all three cases just mentioned, the World Bank, the IMF and the ILO, decision-making procedures are distinctly more efficient, in terms of time needed and resources spent, than in the United Nations. Annual conference time is considerably shorter than the near-interminable General Assembly. Both the World Bank and the ILO have a procedure for selecting draft resolutions to be dealt with at each annual conference which avoids the plethora of resolutions discussed in the UN General Assembly.

Other developments which have had an impact on UN decision making as conceived in the UN Charter have been:

• The rise of operational programmes; these have been particularly associated with the World Bank group, UN Development Programme, UN International Children's Emergency Fund (UNICEF), and others. The governing bodies of these programmes function very much by consensus method.

• The method of holding 'global conferences' under UN auspices;
The first and still probably the most important example of the new series of world conferences is the Stockholm Conference on the Environment held in 1972. It paved the way for permanent machinery in this field (UN Environment Programme, with a secretariat in Nairobi). These conferences have performed a public relations and educational function in areas such as habitat, food, population, and water. However, plans of action, almost ritually adopted, have been only partly implemented, if at all. Yet in many conferences, various government departments have gradually brought their practices and, in some cases, their national legislation into conformity with the recommendations of global UN conferences. It would, however, be useful to have each new proposal for a world conference under UN auspices preceded by rigorous analysis of costs and expected benefits (indeed to have such analysis for all proposals calling for new activities).

• The significance of the voting pattern has changed. The number of abstentions is much larger than in early UN years. If one is in favour one can declare a yes vote or abstain, if one is against one declares a no vote or abstains, and some argue that it does not matter how one votes. Hence, the number of 'explanations of votes' has risen strongly.

- The more subtle use of procedural and parliamentary tactics. Opponents to a motion or proposition have a wide choice of such tactics which include referring to some other body ('ping-pong game'); log-rolling, stirring up opposition, and tabling amendments and/or alternative proposals in the hope of creating confusion, with the result that all proposals are referred to the next session, or to a subsidiary body. Of course, these tactical moves are not essentially different from what occurs in normal parliamentary practice. Yet their abundant use in UN diplomacy comes as a surprise to those who had hoped for idealistic international co-operation.

Changed Environmental Elements

Not only have the impact and composition of actors in UN decision making changed, and their tactics evolved, but also a number of modified environmental elements have put their stamp on decision making and non-decision making in the United Nations. Among these elements the following should be noted (the order does not necessarily indicate their relative importance): increased membership, the rise of nationalism, changed attitudes of the superpowers, change in the level of confidence in international organizations, repetitive debates and politicization.

Increased membership

The membership of the United Nations has more than tripled from the original number of 51 founding members. This has meant that procedures have become more cumbersome and time-consuming. According to an old adage it is difficult to negotiate effectively with more than seven in a room. The drawback can be, and has been, overcome by operating in small groups which report back to larger groups. But perhaps more importantly, the new member States come mostly from cultures which were not necessarily accustomed to the Western democracy type of decision-making processes. The new members from Asia and Africa were not used to making decisions by majority vote. They were more familiar with group caucusing followed by consensus, with often a naturally dominant position of the older or the wiser members of the group. Once in the United Nations they quickly grasped the essence of the voting system and some of them probably believed that the original members would abide by the consequences of majority decision making which they had earlier devised. The pressure for a New International Economic Order was linked to the hope of developing countries that even though UN decisions are not binding, majority decisions made in the United Nations would have a convincing impact on the defeated minority. They soon realized that in sensitive economic or political matters the majority cannot impose its will on the minority, especially if the minority includes important economic powers. The sixth and seventh special sessions of the General

Assembly (1974 and 1975) on the New International Economic Order reflected this ambiguous situation with both sides having to adjust to what was, in fact, a novel situation, both in terms of the political power configuration and in view of the professed objective to negotiate about a great variety of delicate economic matters within a severely limited timespan.

Rise of nationalism

The internationalism which inspired the founding fathers of the United Nations has been widely substituted by a rampant nationalism. In a certain sense the United Nations has reinforced nationalism because countries which have just acquired independence react nationalistically when it is suggested that powers should be handed to some international body. Let me recall a relevant comment: '... Where we should be dealing with all-embracing economic, political and social problems, we discuss minor trade objectives, or small national advantages...We must substitute, before it is too late, imagination for tradition; generosity for shrewdness; understanding for bargaining...wisdom for prejudice...'. These words are not from some vague starry-eyed world reformer but from the hard-boiled Bretton Woods negotiator for the United States in 1944, Harry White. What has happened is that many states prefer to live with some international conflict, possibly because it is the only rallying element in an otherwise difficult domestic situation. In addition, the vagaries of economic life have produced new conflict situations.

Changed attitude of the superpowers

The attitude of the two superpowers vis-à-vis the United Nations is, of course, of great importance. In the case of the USSR there was never much evidence that it was willing to accept supra-national guidance by the world organization. The United States in the early years of the United Nations was distinctly positive about an important role for the organization, a point of view made easier by the majority on which the United States could normally count.[7] Even after the advent of the Cold War when the superpowers were less than ever inclined to take conflicts in which they were themselves involved to the United Nations, the United States proposed bold initiatives through presidential addresses in the General Assembly. President Eisenhower's 'atoms for peace' address to the General Assembly of 1953 which resulted in the creation of the International Atomic Energy Agency (IAEA), and President Kennedy's speech in the General Assembly of 1961, which led to the adoption of the innovative comprehensive resolution on the first UN Development Decade. The mood is now distinctly different. In the economic field the governments of the main industrialized nations are disinclined to take initiatives in the United Nations because there are many alternative organizations in which there is less risk of 'politicization'. In the political area the near-automatism with which each superpower can expect a veto from the other in the Security Council every time its vital interests are deemed to be involved, has had the expected result: the superpowers continue to keep conflicts in which they themselves are involved outside the United Nations.

This lack of idealism and low priority of multilateral arrangements is exemplified by the attitude of the United States towards the new Law of the Sea Treaty: its objections are not so much against the detailed provisions of the treaty but rather a general doctrinaire aversion against giving even limited powers to world institutions. Yet one sees that both the IMF and the World Bank have regained United States favour in as much as they are deemed indispensable actors in dealing with debt and other problems of developing countries (although in this case it is the autonomy of action of these latter countries, not of the United States, which is affected).

The confidence factor

Confidence in international organizations generally and in the United Nations and UN Educational, Scientific and Cultural Organization (UNESCO) in particular has suffered. Stories about the poor performance of the secretariat are popular with governments and with the media; success stories receive little notice. This lack of confidence is related to:

a) Presumed or real declining efficiency of certain international secretariats. 'Presumed or real' because what counts is the impression left with major contributors. If they believe that efficiency has decreased, this belief becomes then an autonomous factor in the attitude of a country vis-à-vis the organization in question.

b) The view, again rightly or wrongly, that a secretariat is biased. This was typically what happened in the case of the UN Conference on Trade and Development (UNCTAD): the United States and other Western countries believe that the reporting and recommendations by the secretariat are inclined towards the views and interests of developing countries, and do not sufficiently take into account the actual facts of a problem or situation.

c) Changed voting power, as a result of which the United States and other Western powers are regularly out-voted by the new majority.

Repetitive debates

The tendency, particularly marked in the General Assembly, to engage year after year in repetitive debate and adoption of the same – often unimplementable – resolutions (on the substance of which there is frequently disagreement) concerning subjects like the Middle East and the problem of apartheid, has harmed the image of the United Nations in certain, especially Western, circles.

Politicization

What is commonly called politicization is not a new factor in UN decision making but is in some of the specialized agencies. The concept of politicization is ambiguous. It seems to cover three types of events:

a) the predominance of political debate in an organization, combined with the presumed use by certain governments of such debates for their own political advantage;
b) the rise in the technical specialized agencies of debate on political issues and the consequent introduction and eventual adoption of resolutions on such political issues;
c) the exaggerated emphasis – contrary to the organization's Charter – on certain particular objectives or activities by the executive head of an organization (sometimes combined with arbitrary or nepotistic rule also in staff appointment matters, and mismanagement generally).

Politicization is also reflected in the habit of making speeches for 'domestic consumption'. Politicization of UNESCO was presumably the main reason why the United States withdrew. The Soviet bloc countries accuse the ILO of being involved in a different kind of politicization: 'Since their elaboration in 1919 the ILO's basic concept and structure have remained essentially unchanged. The Organization virtually ignores the fact of admission of socialist and developing countries to its membership. By following its old course, the ILO in effect serves the interests of only one socio-political system, that of capitalism, in an attempt to impose its will and ways on other States'.[8]

Improvements in UN Decision Making

There seem to be two direct ways to implement possible improvements:

- the management route; by adopting certain presumed improvements in the decision-making process,
- the restructuring route; by endeavouring to streamline and simplify the organizational set-up of the United Nations and the system of specialized agencies; the term restructuring is sometimes used for this type of exercise.

Improving the decision-making process (the 'management route')

Over the years a lot of suggestions and proposals have been made to improve the decision-making process in the United Nations, both in several of the organizations and in numerous private conferences, such as those sponsored by the Stanley Foundation.

Recently, a meeting of former Presidents of the General Assembly made recommendations concerning the rationalization of the procedures of the GA.[9] They recommended, for example, that items which are 'no longer relevant' should be eliminated from the General Assembly's agenda and that the General Committee should 'scrutinize the draft agenda more closely '. I doubt whether in the absence of a complete change of spirit among member States this can be realized, since a feeling of general tolerance, indeed perhaps nonchalance, appears to dominate about the question of acceptability of agenda items. The assembly presidents also recommend a reduction of documentation, specifically that 'the General Assembly should not automatically, upon the conclusion of an item, request the Secretary General for the submission of a report'. Presumably, a reduction in documents can only be achieved by severe self-restraint shown by governments, and by trying to eliminate some of the periodic reporting which is no longer necessary.

There are, no doubt, other possible improvements that could be made in the decision-making process of the General Assembly and other UN agencies:

- Too much time is now spent on speech-making. As a result less time is available for negotiations. An effort could be made to restrict debates rigorously. As at the ILO and the World Health Organization (WHO), statements in general debates at the General Assembly could be limited to 15 minutes. In agencies like UNCTAD, an effort should be made to separate speech-making and negotiation, somewhat along the lines of the procedure at the IMF and the World Bank.

- It has become general practice for the secretariat to put up a 'statement of financial implications' for any new proposal requiring study or action. It might be worth considering, in addition to this, a statement of 'cost-effectiveness' or of 'cost-benefit'. In other words, one should look at not only the expected costs, but also, and especially, at the expected benefits. If such an assessment were systematically undertaken, it could become an important factor in restoring confidence in the United Nations as an organization which will only engage in new activities that are really useful.

- The worst period for engaging in group negotiations may be over. This period was exemplified by the well-known dichotomy in UNCTAD: the group of 77 was unified concerning a set of maximum demands, and the Group of developed countries (Group B) settled for a minimum response, followed by difficult negotiations between the two groups whose negotiators had to go back for each modification to their group as a whole.[10] Negotiations in small contact groups without a rigid mandate have demonstrably given optimal results. This is how the UN Special Fund in 1957/58 and the complex, far-reaching issue of the Law of the Sea Conference were negotiated. The technique of 'small *ad hoc* fire brigades' should be used more often and earlier in the negotiating process.

- It might be worthwhile to endeavour to improve the 'definition-making' process. Various terms, including 'peace', 'racism' and 'imperialism' have been used in the United Nations in a loose manner. Certain resolutions using these terms have had a negative impact in the United States and elsewhere. Ideally, the United Nations could establish a 'Committee on Definitions' to which controversial texts could be referred, with – if necessary – a long delay in voting and possibly the Sixth (Legal) Committee of the General Assembly could be given a task in this respect. However, such a committee does not belong to the realm of practical possibilities. Alternatively, the International Court of Justice could be approached more often for an advisory opinion on some concept or definition in a draft resolution. What is needed is a face-saving and time-gaining procedure in an otherwise intractable situation.

Streamlining the organizational structure of the United Nations and the specialized agencies (the 'restructuring route')

A better and more streamlined structure would make an important contribution to more efficient decision making. It would avoid the duplication which causes both loss of time and resources. In the United Nations, restructuring efforts (the last occurred in 1979 after the report of the Group of 25) have not yielded many results. The creation of the post of Director-General for Development and International Economic Co-operation has added to, rather than diminished, the complexity of the UN organizational set-up. The UN telephone directory, which still serves as the United Nations' organization chart, lists the Director-General for Development and International Economic Co-operation immediately after the Secretary-General and his office. He is presumed to be, but not officially recognized as, the number two in the secretariat. When the Administrative Committee for Co-ordination was, in the absence of the Secretary-General, to be chaired by the then newly-appointed Director-General, the heads of the specialized agencies protested: in their view, in the absence of the Secretary-General, the most senior Director-General of a specialized agency should preside. The streamlining of ECOSOC especially by holding shorter subject-oriented sessions as recommended by the restructuring resolution of 1977 no. 32/197 has hardly materialized. There is probably 're-structuring-fatigue' in the United Nations slightly comparable to aid and other fatigues. Yet some simple steps could improve the situation. Thus, combined sessions of ECOSOC and the UNCTAD Board for the many items which overlap in their respective agendas could be a modest step towards greater efficiency in the economic and social field and towards a restoration of confidence in ECOSOC. If this were successful then some of the subordinate bodies of ECOSOC and IUNCTAD could also be de facto merged.

Ideally, ECOSOC should assume the role of an economic security council, ready to deal both with any situation requiring immediate attention in the economic field and with the long-term problems of poverty in developing countries. Thus, the arrangements and structure for dealing with the emergency needs of Africa could perhaps have been created more smoothly if ECOSOC could have met and acted quickly, just as the Security Council is supposed to do in political crisis situations. Yet the organization created to deal with the food emergency in Africa (UN Office for Emergency Operations in Africa, OEOA) is functioning well, showing that, despite constitutional constraints (between the United Nations and individual governments), the United Nations could respond efficiently to an emergency.[11]

Also, ECOSOC could revive an economic policy committee, along the lines of a similar committee which it created in the early years. Such an economic policy committee could look at the overall world economic situation (somewhat like the Economic Policy Committee of OECD) in relation to the economic situation in its member countries. An alternative would be to 'upgrade' the existing Committee for Development Planning (CDP) (including a change of name). Not much use is now made of the CDP, which is a pity since in the earlier period it played, for example, a key role in drafting the strategy for the Second Development Decade. In any transformation of the CDP into an Economic Policy Committee the question will arise whether the members should be independent experts, as is the case at present, or high government officials in charge of economic policy (as at the OECD Economic Policy Committee), or perhaps a mix of government officials and independent experts, which is done in the UN Commission on Transnational Corporations.

In the political field, if efforts to reduce the number of repetitious resolutions was successful, the Special Political Committee of ECOSOC could probably be dissolved and its remaining business taken back by the First Committee. Similarly, the Second (Economic) and Third (Social and Humanitarian) Committees of the General Assembly might eventually be merged if they could eliminate repetitious items and structure their consideration of various programmes in such a way that, in line with the biennial budget concept, each programme is considered only once every two years.[12]

It is tempting to reflect on a different set-up of specialized agencies and other similar UN organizations. Each agency has more or less active support by specific bureaucracies in the various capitals of the world. That being the case, ideas for streamlining or merging must be considered, at this time, as unrealistic. Yet one could conceive of more integrated clusters of specialized agencies and certain UN organs dealing with related subjects:

i) Food and Agricultural Organization (FAO), WHO, ILO, IAEA, UN Industrial Development Organization (UNIDO), and other parts of the United Nations deal with basic natural or human resources. A joint advisory council, for whose composition different formulae are conceivable, could result in better co-ordination and co-operation than is the case at present. For example, the UNIDO, after several years as a UN branch, became a specialized agency, yet the opportunity to merge with either the ILO or with FAO lapsed unnoticed.

ii) The World Bank, IMF, UNCTAD and General Agreement on Tariffs and Trade (GATT) deal with trade and finance. The strong link between the worlds of trade and finance is one of the re-discovered revelations of today. A joint advisory council for trade and finance matters might be constituted serving the agencies in this field. An eventual merger of UNCTAD and GATT, although at the same time preserving the autonomy of GATT, should be considered.

iii) Almost every agency deals in one way or another with human resources. The UN Development Programme (UNDP) prides itself on being specialized in the development of human resources. An inter-agency advisory board on human resources, possibly chaired by the Administrator of UNDP, could lead to a better co-ordinated approach to the human side of economic and social development.

There are also some notable absences in the present structure of the UN system:

Energy. While energy in all its respects is of undeniable importance, the subject is dealt with by a great many organs. The International Atomic Energy Agency deals, of course, with nuclear energy; other aspects of energy are the object of activities in the UN Secretariat in New York in the regional commissions, and – strangely – in an institution like UN Institute for Training and Research (UNITAR), which has set up an efficient data bank covering a gap felt by private business for tar sands oil. A single agency for energy would be logical, although a careful cost-effectiveness analysis should prevent any premature decision. A World Bank energy affiliate could also be considered.

Human misery. The United Nations would seem a logical place to have a central office dealing with the various calamities which can befall mankind: physical disasters, other emergencies such as those resulting from civil war, human rights violations, refugee problems. There is a UN High Commissioner for Refugees, a UN Disaster Relief Office, of limited size, and also an Human Rights Division. Efforts to create a UN High Commissioner for Human Rights have failed. Would it not make sense to set up a single Office, headed by a (High) Commissioner to deal with all aspects of human misery? There is, in relation to famine in Africa, a cluster of agencies working together under the auspices of the UN Office of Emergency Assistance to Africa. This cluster includes UNICEF, World Food Programme, International Fund for Agricultural Development (IFAD), International Development Association (IDA) and the World Bank, and could be the precursor of a more permanent mechanism.

Research and fact-finding. There are, probably, too many UN research institutes. Some of them, like UN Research Institute for Disarmament

(UNIDIR) and WIDER (World Institute for Development Economics Research) have been founded thanks to the generosity of a single government. The UN University and UN Institute for Training and Research overlap in certain respects. A streamlined set-up of research institutes in the United Nations, and ideally in the UN system as a whole, would also assist in providing a better flow of reports and facts to the decision makers. Better fact-finding is generally needed, as stressed by the Secretary-General in his Annual Report 1985.

Conclusions

All these possible attempts to reduce UN inefficiency or suboptimal decision making are bound to fail if there is a lack of real will for international co-operation, and willingness to accept supranational guidance in certain situations (there will, of course, always be escape-clauses). To achieve this co-operation for such a specific purpose it will be necessary to engage in research into the cultural, psychological and semantic constraints of international co-operation.

Even if there were to be considerable improvement in both the management of UN decision-making processes and in the structure of the UN system, it remains doubtful whether international co-operation would gain very much in the absence of a real will to accept the consequences of such co-operation, namely the diminishing of national sovereign powers.

The question arises whether deeper insights into the widespread resistance to yielding parts of national power to a supranational authority are needed. The answer would seem to be in the affirmative. This unavoidably seems to mean research into the cultural and psychological barriers to international co-operation. Is there something like a psychopathological personality of nations? Do nations feel persecuted, or claustrophobic, and hence say 'no' to many proposals tending to diminish their already uncertain powers? Do the largest powers have a 'large power complex' making them indifferent to the needs of smaller countries? There has been little systematic research into these matters, even though the individual negotiating styles of particular nations have been researched.[13]

Notes

1) See C.F. Alger, *The United Nations in Historical Perspective: What have we Learned about Peacebuilding?*, Paper for the UN University Global Seminar on International Organizations, Hakone, Japan, 9–15 September 1985. Also I.L. Claude Jr, *Swords Into Plowshares. The Problems and Progress of International Organization*, Random House, New York, 1964.

2) W.R. Sharp, *The UN Economic and Social Council*, New York, 1969, p.3; E. Luard, *The Evolution of International Organizations*, New York 1966, pp. 248–249.

3) See Johan Kaufmann, *United Nations Decision Making*, Chapter 10, Sijthoff Noordhoff, Alphen a/d Rijn, 1980.

4) *Ibid*; see also for some early ideas the Bruce Committee Report of the League of Nations – Monthly Summary of the *League of Nations*, August 1939.

5) C.F. Alger, *op. cit.* note 1.

6) While I would like to see the non-governmental organizations associated with all decisions in the implementation of which they are involved, I do not believe it would be constructive to have them associated in actual legislative processes. This is advocated by Marc Nerfin in 'The Future of the United Nations System', in: *Development Dialogue*, 1985, p. 1 (also in 45 *IFDA Dossier*, Jan/Feb. 1985). He proposes that in addition to a *Prince Chamber* which would represent government, there should be a *Merchant Chamber* representing economic interest groupings and a *Citizen Chamber* to speak for the people and their associations. My concern is that such additional chambers, even if they would act only in an advisory capacity, would provide easy excuses for governments to delay action.

7) The evolution of United States viewpoints regarding the United Nations is well described in Thomas M. Franck, *Nation against Nation*, Oxford University Press, 1985.

8) Declaration of the socialist countries on the situation in the International Labour Organization, annexed to *UN Doc.* A/40/458.

9) See *UN Doc.* A/40/377.

10) Cf. Johan Kaufmann, *Conference Diplomacy*, 1968, pp. 149–152.

11) See for constructive suggestions on how to deal with famine *Famine, a Man-made Disaster? A Report for the Independent Commission on International Humanitarian Issues*, Pan Books, London, 1985.

12) A promising effort in this direction was made with General Assembly resolution 39/219 (1984) on the biennial programme of work for the General Assembly second committee.

13) This paper concentrated on some specific selected aspects of United Nations negotiations and decision-making. On the occasion of the United Nations' fortieth anniversary there have been several thought-provoking reflections on the United Nations' past and future. In addition to Marc Nerfin's article referred to in note 6, I mention: M. Bertrand, *Some Reflections on Reform in the United Nations*, Report of the Joint Inspection Unit, JIU/REP/85/9, Geneva, 1985; Ph. de Seynes, 'Real opportunities ahead', in: *Development Forum*, November 1985; John E. Fobes, 'The Future of the United Nations System', in: 51 *IFDA Dossier, January/February 1986*. On the lessons to be learned from IMF practices see Frederick K. Lister, *Decision-making Strategies for International*

Organizations, Monograph Series in World Affairs, Volume 20, Book Denver, Denver, Colorado, 1984. Successive annual reports of the present Secretary-General, Mr J. Perez de Cuellar, have offered important proposals for improvements in the UN decision-making system.

4 The Role of the United Nations in the Development of International Law

Nico Schrijver*

Introduction

'The United Nations is the most concentrated assault on moral reality in the history of free institutions, and it does not do to ignore that fact or, worse, to get used to it', writes William Buckley in his book *United Nations Journal. A Delegate's Odyssey*.[1] On the other hand, the Secretary-General of the United Nations, Perez de Cuellar, has stated that 'the United Nations is the principal instrument for the community of nations to guide international life according to standards which all have accepted in agreeing to the Charter, and to undertake the law-making activities which are essential to orderly growth and development'.[2]

The division of opinion on the role of the United Nations in the establishment of moral standards is reflected in an equally sharp division of opinion concerning its role in the development of international law. Schwebel, a former legal advisor of the US State Department and currently one of the judges on the International Court of Justice (ICJ) wrote in 1979: '...what States *do* is more important than

* *Nico Schrijver* is a lecturer in public international law and international institutions at the Institute of Social Studies, The Hague, and a member of the (Dutch) National Advisory Council for International Development Co-operation. He was a member of The Netherlands' delegation to the 33rd UN General Assembly in 1978, representing Dutch youth organizations. He has published in the fields of international law, international organization and on the legal aspects of development and international security.

what they say. It is especially more important than what they may say in a General Assembly context'.[3] According to Bedjaoui, a former Algerian government minister and Ambassador to the United Nations and now also a judge at the ICJ, resolutions have become 'the modern source' of international law.[4] Thus, he seems to suggest that resolutions have displaced treaties and custom as the main sources of international law.

From these statements it can be seen that the role of the United Nations in the development of international standards is under attack but also that it is defended with at least equal force. In this chapter it is not possible to analyse the merits of these opinions. The intention is rather to present some facts and analysis relevant to the debate by submitting, firstly, a review of the role of the United Nations in the codification of international law; secondly, some observations on the role of UN resolutions in the development of international law; and thirdly, a brief examination of the role of the International Court of Justice in the consolidation and development of international law.

Treaties and the Development of International Law

Article 13 of the UN Charter calls upon the UN General Assembly to initiate studies and make recommendations for encouraging 'the progressive development of international law and its codification'. This was the first time in history that such a provision has been included in the constitution of a major international organization. As early as 1947, the General Assembly (GA) established the International Law Commission (ILC) as a subsidiary organ for the discharge of these responsibilities. The Statute of the ILC provides that the Commission as a whole should represent 'the main forms of civilization and the principal legal systems of the world' (Art. 8).

Soon after the adoption of the UN Charter the question of how to interpret the terms 'progressive development' and 'codification' was raised. The Statute of the ILC provides some help in answering this question. Article 15 uses the former term 'for convenience as meaning the preparation of draft conventions on subjects which have not yet been regulated by international law or in regions to which the law has not yet been sufficiently developed in the practice of States', and the latter is assumed to mean 'the more precise formulation and systematization of international law in fields where there already has been extensive State practice, precedent and doctrine.' To put it concisely: progressive development essentially aims at developing new law – *lex ferenda*; codification essentially aims at clarifying existing law – *lex lata*.

This differentiation, however, soon proved to be impracticable. The ILC became particularly aware of this problem when drafting the four Law of the Sea Conventions during the 1950s.[5] For a sound and complete codification of the law of the sea, the Commission had to deal both with a more precise formulation and systematization of already existing rules, for example, in the fields of freedom of navigation and sovereignty over the territorial sea, and it also had to devise new rules in the fields of such relatively new problems as the exploitation of the mineral resources of the continental shelf and the protection of the living resources of the high seas. But in both cases a mixture of 'codification' and 'progressive development' was involved and it was often not possible to draw a clear line between the two.

Despite these difficulties the ILC did succeed in producing a considerable number of draft conventions on important legal issues in international relations during the first three decades of its existence.[6] On the basis of the ILC drafts, diplomatic conferences convened by the United Nations have adopted a number of multilateral conventions including: four Law of the Sea Conventions (1958), a Convention on Diplomatic Relations (1961) and another on Consular Relations (1963), the Vienna Convention on the Law of Treaties (1969), two Conventions on Succession of States in Respect of Treaties (1978) and in Respect of State Property, Archives and Debts (1983), as well as one on Treaties Concluded Between States and International Organizations or Between Two or More International Organizations (1986).

These are impressive results indeed. It has been stated, however, that, during the last decade, the ILC has lost its pre-eminent role in the development of international law. In a report of the United Nations Institute for Training and Research (UNITAR), entitled 'The International Law Commission: the Need for a New Direction', it is concluded that the ILC 'is no longer playing the central role in the law-making process that it could and should play'.[7] Several factors causing this alleged decline of influence of the Commission are suggested. The ILC is said to have failed to accommodate itself to the fundamental changes in the world community it is supposed to serve, especially in connection with the emergence of the majority of newly-independent States. Furthermore, the ILC is deemed to have paid much more attention to codification, having focused attention primarily on topics of traditional international law (diplomatic and consular relations, law of treaties, state responsibility), than to progressive development. This as the result of an attempt to avoid political issues.

On one hand, these conclusions may seem to be somewhat unfair. The ILC's draft conventions certainly embody a large number of innovative elements which can be characterized as progressive development. In the case of the Vienna Convention on the Law of Treaties (1969), these include a reformulation of the *clausula rebus sic stantibus* − a fundamental change of circumstances which, under very strict conditions, can even supersede the sacrosanct rule of *pacta sunt servanda* (treaties have to be observed) − and of the concept of *jus cogens*, notably that a treaty is void or becomes void if it conflicts with a peremptory norm of general international law. On the other hand, it could indeed be claimed that the recent contributions of the ILC to the development of international law pertaining to such important topics as commodities, financial and monetary relations, and environmental protection, which could very well lend themselves to progressive development, is negligible. It is indeed striking, that the ILC had no part at all in the drafting of the new UN Convention on the Law of the Sea (1982). But it should be realized that it is not the ILC itself which should be held entirely responsible for this state of affairs. The Commission can only act under the instruction of the General Assembly, and it is the Assembly which prevented it from dealing with politically sensitive legal issues, confining it to more technical areas of international law. Thus, considering the political and economic interests involved in reviewing the principles and rules of the law of the sea, the General Assembly decided in 1973 not to entrust the ILC with this task but directly to convene a UN Conference on the Law of the Sea (UNCLOS-III), in which all member States could participate.

It should be noted that in the UN system the ILC, the General Assembly and its Sixth (Legal) Committee play an important role in the development and codification of international law, but they do not have the monopoly over it. As early as 1946 the UN Commission on Human Rights was established in order, among other purposes, to submit proposals for an international bill of human rights. This permanent Commission performed its task very energetically and soon after its establishment it proposed the adoption of a Universal Declaration of Human Rights to the General Assembly. By 1954, the Commission had drawn up two Human Rights Covenants: one on civil and political rights, another on social, cultural and economic rights. Although the competition between the two major rival social systems had some beneficial effects on the drafting of human rights law (notably the inclusion of social and economic rights and the right to self-determination), the Cold War and the emergence of the newly-independent nations delayed and complicated its completion as well. As a result, it took another twelve years before the political organs of the United Nations were in a position to adopt these Covenants in 1966. In that year, the General Assembly also established the permanent UN Commission on International Trade Law (UNCITRAL) to deal with legal aspects of the sale of goods, international payments and commercial arbitration. In addition, the UN Conference on Trade and Development (UNCTAD) has served as the forum for international negotiations on individual commodity agreements and an Agreement on the Establishment of a Common Fund for Commodities (1980). Also in the context of UNCTAD a number of international agreements has been concluded related to such topics as world shipping and transit trade of land-locked states.

Apart from these permanent bodies, the General Assembly has also set up several *ad hoc* organs entrusted with the task of drawing up specific legal documents. In 1958, the Committee on the Peaceful Uses of Outer Space was established (from 1960 as a permanent body), the work of which resulted in a number of important treaties on the exploration and use of outer space, including the moon and other celestial bodies. In 1978, the Commission on Human Rights established an *ad hoc*, open-ended Working Group to draft a convention against torture. On 10 December 1984, the General Assembly adopted the Convention Against Torture and Other Cruel, Inhuman or Degrading Treatment or Punishment and opened it for signature, ratification and accession. Moreover, arms control treaties have been concluded within the framework of other UN activities. Reference can be made to the Treaty on the Non-Proliferation of Nuclear Weapons (1968), the Sea-Bed Arms Control Treaty (1971) and the Convention on the Prohibition of Military or Any Other Hostile Use of Environmental Modification Techniques (1977).

Apart from the law-making activities of the UN proper, reference should be made to the work of the 'specialized agencies'. Several among these institutions have developed and codified substantial bodies of law in their fields of competence, such as the World Health Organization (WHO), the International Labour Organization (ILO), the World Intellectual Property Organization (WIPO) and the Universal Postal Union (UPU).

In one of these, the ILO, the treaty-making activities are quite unique compared with those in other parts of the UN system and deserve some discussion:[8]

1. The International Labour Conference has a tripartite composition, including State and non-State representatives (employers' and workers' delegates);

2. Upon adoption by at least a two-thirds majority of the Conference, all member States – including those whose government delegates did not vote in favour of the Convention – are under the obligation to submit the newly-adopted conventions to the competent national authorities within a period of 12 or 18 months for consideration of legislative or other action. They must inform the Director-General of the ILO of the action taken in this respect;

3. A State which ratifies an ILO Convention cannot make any reservation. This is a very striking exception to the rules on reservations as embodied in the Vienna Convention on the Law of Treaties. This is because the adoption of a Convention is supposed to be the act of the entire Conference, which includes non-State delegates as well. The tripartite composition implies for similar reasons that State Parties to a Convention are not free to agree *inter se* on an interpretation or revision of a Convention;

4. For a State ratifying a Convention there is a continuing process of supervision. Reports have to be submitted annually to the ILO and there is a complaints procedure. Even for a State not ratifying a Convention there is a procedure of regular inquiry.

   Apart from Conventions, the ILO can also adopt Recommendations. The latter are not binding, but are intended to provide guidance for national policy, legislation and practice. From 1919 to 1986, 162 Conventions and 172 Recommendations have been adopted by the ILO on trade union rights, elimination of discrimination in employment, forced labour, employment of women and children, migrant workers, etc.

The progressive law-making procedures of the ILO exerted an influence upon the practice of other international organizations, such as the UN Educational, Scientific and Cultural Organization (UNESCO) and WHO.

Codification efforts have also been made outside the United Nations at the non-governmental level. The most well-known example is the work of the International Committee of the Red Cross in the field of international humanitarian law and the law of warfare.

In the post-war period, the codification of international law has made unprecedented progress. Some 350 multilateral treaties have been adopted under the auspices of the United Nations. Substantial bodies of law in the field of human rights, diplomatic relations, law of the sea, law of treaties have been further developed and codified. As a result, it could even be claimed that treaty law has begun to replace customary law as the dominant source of international law.

Developing countries have increasingly been participating in the drafting process of treaties. In the pre-UN period, treaties rarely had more than 15 parties. By contrast, most UN conventions nowadays have over 60 parties; some very important ones even over 100. Yet, traditionally, developing countries have a suspicious attitude towards treaties, because they tend to consider them as reflecting *status quo* law. In colonial times but also during and after the attainment of independence, they frequently experienced treaties as instruments of suppression and exploitation and labelled these as 'unequal treaties'.[9] The UN Charter shows an awareness of this concern: while the Covenant of the League of Nations still demanded 'a scrupulous respect for all treaty obligations', the UN Charter does not repeat this phrase and seems to give priority to 'justice' over strict respect for the rule of law where it declares in its preamble that the peoples of the United Nations are determined 'to establish conditions under which justice and respect for the obligations arising from treaties and other sources of international law can be maintained.'

Although from a historical point of view the suspicious attitude of developing countries towards treaties is quite understandable, they are now slowly beginning to recognize the role of treaties as instruments of both change and co-operation between States. Apart from this, it should be realized that in certain fields such as arms control, *status quo* oriented treaties can have a positive influence on the development of stable international relations. Yet, in spite of increasing participation of developing countries in the treaty-making process and in spite of the adoption in the law of treaties of innovative versions of the *clausula rebus sic stantibus* and *jus cogens*, treaty law is still frequently stigmatized as *status quo* law which tends to serve the interests of the Western countries. Bedjaoui represents this view when he observes: '...for a number of legal and political reasons the developing countries are not on an equal footing with the others in the negotiation and conclusion of treaties. Since international law is still characterized by formalism in the emergence and application of its rules, treaties are not always a true manifestation of free will. They can often be the result of pressures, of constraints or of different conditions that are not met at the moment of their conclusion'. Accordingly, he concludes: 'The Third World thus holds the method of convention in esteem, although not unqualified esteem... Nonetheless, it cannot be denied that the technique of the resolution of the international organization holds a greater attraction for the Third World.'[10] To underpin his conclusion he refers to the flexibility and rapidity of resolutions and to the security they can give to the developing countries as a result of their majority position. However, resolutions do not have the same legal force in international law as treaties.

Resolutions and the Development of International Law

In the pre-UN era, the term 'resolution' was normally used in the sense of a binding decision taken in the context of an international conference (e.g., Concert of Europe) or an international organization. Usually these conferences and organizations took their decisions unanimously, so that a resolution could be seen as a simplified form of inter-State agreement.[11]

During the San Francisco Conference in 1945, some small and medium powers attempted to invest the General Assembly with extensive powers. The delegation of the Philippines even proposed to entrust the General Assembly with legislative powers to enact rules of international law which would become effective and binding upon the members of the United Nations after their approval by a majority of the Security Council. All these proposals, however, were rejected. The Security Council was invested with the primary responsibility for the maintenance and restoration of international peace and security and was empowered to take binding decisions under Articles 24–25 and under Chapter VII of the UN Charter. Articles 10 to 14, in which the general competence of the General Assembly is outlined, refer solely to recommendations.

In the UN Charter itself, the term 'resolution' is not used at all. Reference is only made to 'recommendations' and 'decisions'. For UN purposes resolutions are formal, written texts in which the conclusion of debates are formulated and the (unanimous or majority) views of the organization are expressed. They cover both binding decisions and recommendations.

As regards binding decisions, it can be observed by their contents that their contribution to the development of international law has been rather limited. Ironically, a number of recommendations - in particular certain resolutions of the General Assembly of the United Nations – appear to have contributed much more to the progressive development of international law. Such resolutions have been referred to by some authors as 'soft' law: something between binding 'hard' law and non-binding recommendations, something less than law but more than mere moral or political commitments ('non-law').

It is often difficult to distinguish between existing, positive law (*lex lata*), law in the making (*lex ferenda*) and politics. As Abi-Saab put it: 'In reality, law does not come out at social nothingness, nor does it come with a 'big bang'. In most cases,

39

it is a progressive and imprescriptible growth over a large 'grey zone' separating emerging social values from the well established legal rule; a zone which is very difficult (and sometimes even impossible) to divide *a posteriori* between the two'.[12]

Opinions on the precise legal status of General Assembly resolutions and their contribution to the development of international law differ widely. These opinions range from theories according to which resolutions could be considered as the primary source of international law to the position that they should be denied any legal significance beyond their formal status of mere recommendations.

In an attempt to clarify their legal status, one should keep in mind, firstly, that most resolutions have nothing to do with international law at all. They have quite often a purely political or factual content. Only those which are normative in scope and clearly purport to formulate principles and/or rules of international law are legally relevant and potentially capable of contributing to the development of international law. Secondly, even the legal value of resolutions of the latter kind may vary widely from case to case. Verwey has inventively suggested nine inter-related variables by which the potential legal significance of a particular resolution can be analysed and tested, including the form, wording, degree of specification, circumstances of adoption, and monitoring and control procedures.[13]

Below, an attempt will be made – though certainly not in an exhaustive manner – to summarize and classify in general terms the legally most relevant categories of UN resolutions. The order of listing is not arbitrary but tries to indicate the successive degrees of legal value which can be attached to them. Eight groups of decreasing legal significance can be identified.

Binding decisions addressed to member States

Under Article 25 of the UN Charter, the members of the United Nations agree to accept and carry out the decisions of the Security Council in accordance with the Charter. Under Chapter VII the Security Council is authorized to command collective measures in the case of a threat to peace, breach of peace or act of aggression. These collective measures can be of a non-military or military nature. Non-military measures may include economic sanctions or severance of diplomatic relations. Military measures – the ultimate recourse of the system of collective security – may include collective military action against an aggressor. So far, the Security Council has commanded only non-military measures: a trade embargo against South Rhodesia (1966–1979) and an arms embargo against South Africa (1977 up to the present).

Apart from the Security Council, certain 'specialized agencies' can take majority decisions which, in principle, are binding upon its members, except when they notify the agency in question of their rejection or reservations (the so-called 'opting-out procedure'). For example, the World Health Organization employs this procedure with respect to its 'regulations'. The 'international standards' of the International Civil Aviation Organization give rise to binding obligations for all member States, in the case of the Rules of the Air, even without the possibility of opting out.

Binding internal and 'household' decisions with external effects

Each organization is competent to regulate its own internal matters: for example, admission or expulsion of members, the establishment and composition of subsidiary organs (ILC, UNCTAD) and their rules of procedure, the establishment of the budget and the assessment of the contribution to be paid by individual member States. Such resolutions can be more than mere 'house-keeping' resolutions and can have important external effects. It is through a binding decision by the General Assembly under Article 17 of the UN Charter that the United Nations currently devotes almost one-third of the regular budget to economic, social and humanitarian affairs. In 1966 the General Assembly decided to terminate the Mandate over South West Africa which had been given by the League of Nations to South Africa in 1920, and placed the territory under the direct responsibility of the United Nations. In 1967 the Assembly subsequently delegated, within its own rules of procedure, legislative and administrative authority over the territory to a subsidiary organ, the UN Council for Namibia. Also other internal decisions on organizational matters may have important external effects, such as those establishing 'peace-keeping forces' (operating in e.g., Egypt, the Congo and Lebanon) or extending the competence of the UN High Commissioner for Refugees (UNHCR).

In this latter case, the UN General Assembly adopted the Statute of the Office of the UNHCR, which was established as a subsidiary organ of the General Assembly in 1950. Without formally amending this Statute, the functions and powers of the UNHCR have been considerably broadened by successive GA resolutions. Today, they include international protection of refugees, assistance to refugees, and, in general, the competence to deal with 'problems of refugees and displaced persons wherever they occur'. The definition of the term 'refugees' has been continuously broadened beyond the 'mandate refugees'. In addition, 'displaced persons' are mentioned side by side with refugees, even persons displaced within their own country.

Apart from operational action and material assistance, the UNHCR also plays a key role in promoting the conclusion and adoption of international refugee conventions and in monitoring their implementation.

Thus, by way of successive resolutions, the General Assembly has actively interpreted the original mandate of the UNCHR. The scope of the High Commissioner's competence *ratione personae* and *ratione materiae* has been extended in order – in the words of Prince Sadruddin Agha Khan who served as the High Commissioner from 1965 to 1977 – 'to match the increasing humanitarian problems of today's world'.[14]

Resolutions can further explain and specify principles and rules of treaties as, for example, those of the UN Charter. During the 1945 San Francisco Conference it was already recognized that 'in the course of the operation from day to day of the various organs of the Organization, it is inevitable that each organ will interpret such parts of the Charter as are applicable to its particular function. This process is inherent in the functioning of any body which operates under an instrument defining its functioning powers'.[15]

Indeed, a large number of UN resolutions incorporate general or specific interpretations of the UN Charter. Quite often these are extensive interpretations and sometimes they come close to *de facto* amendments to it. Provisions of this kind include clarifications of the constitutional powers and functions of a particular organ as well as interpretations of substantive provisions.

An example, be it a controversial one, of the first category is the Uniting for Peace Resolution (1950), in which the General Assembly endowed itself with the power to recommend, under certain circumstances, collective measures aimed at maintaining or restoring international peace in case the Security Council is unable to perform its task because of a lack of unanimity among its permanent members. In the case of a breach of the peace or act of aggression these measures may even include a recommendation to use armed force to restore international peace. According to the opponents of this Resolution (in particular the Soviet Union, which has called it a 'Disuniting for War Resolution') the General Assembly has acted *ultra vires* (beyond its competence) by adopting this Resolution. In practice, however, the Resolution has been invoked and applied several times and, in 1956 and 1967, even at the initiative of the Soviet Union itself.[16]

A first example to be mentioned in the category of interpretations of substantive provisions is the Universal Declaration of Human Rights, adopted in 1948 and elaborating on the few Charter provisions on human rights. The Universal Declaration itself was proclaimed as a 'common standard of achievement'. In 1968, the UN Conference on Human Rights in Tehran adopted a resolution in which it was stated that the Universal Declaration of Human Rights 'constitutes an obligation for the members of the international community'. Although the Declaration still has the status of a recommendation, today most of the norms contained in this Declaration are accepted as binding legal norms. The Declaration on the Granting of Independence to Colonial Countries and Peoples (1960) is often referred to as another example. Indeed, in its paragraph 1 it is declared that: 'The subjection of peoples to alien subjugation, domination and exploitation constitutes a denial of fundamental human rights, is contrary to the Charter of the United Nations and is an impediment to the promotion of world peace and co-operation.' However, the UN Charter itself does not – to say the least – imply this view, since it certainly did not outlaw colonialism immediately. In fact, on the contrary, it even legalized the colonial system by instituting the trusteeship system and by not going further than the prescription of guidelines for a just colonial policy towards the non-self-governing territories. Today, the Decolonization Declaration of 1960 is widely seen as the legal basis for outlawing colonialism and as having *de facto* amended or otherwise superseded the UN Charter in this respect. The Declaration on Principles of International Law concerning Friendly Relations and Co-operation among States in Accordance with the Charter of the United Nations (1970) is proclaimed as an interpretation of the UN Charter, as its title reflects. It is widely considered as a legal document of the utmost importance when it comes to clarifying and elaborating on the meaning of the principles of the Charter.[17]

If such interpretative resolutions are – or by subsequent repetition become – unambiguously and widely supported, they can be regarded as an authoritative interpretation of the UN Charter.

Resolutions as evidence of customary international law: declaratory resolutions

Customary international law is listed, after treaties, as the second source of international law enumerated in the Statute of the International Court of Justice. It is referred to as 'international custom, as evidence of a general practice accepted as law' (Art. 38). The traditional view is that a customary rule must be based on:

a) 'a constant and uniform usage' (as the ICJ put it in the *Asylum* case of 1950) or – as stated later – at least without major inconsistencies in practice (*Fisheries* case, 1951); and

b) the conviction felt by States that a certain form of conduct is required by international law; the legal name given to this 'psychological' element in the formation of customary law is *opinio juris*.[18]

Uncertainty has always existed as to where to look for evidence of customary law. Apart from treaties and other manifestations of State practice, UN resolutions can be considered as providing evidence of customary law in so far as they identify, specify and confirm rules of customary law. As Bowett puts it: 'While they cannot create direct legal obligations for member States they can embody a consensus of opinion about what the law is, so that, indirectly, they become evidence of international law'.[19]

The sets of resolutions on the principle of self-determination or the duty of non-intervention are examples of such 'declaratory resolutions', resolutions which confirm principles or rules of customary international law.

The General Assembly has devised a number of techniques to emphasize and reinforce the legal value of its normative resolutions, in which important principles are included. For instance, by calling its resolutions 'declarations'. The use of the term 'declaration' suggests that the General Assembly is concerned with an act of the confirmation or codification of already existing, customary principles of international law rather than with the creation of new ones. It is questionable, however, to what extent declarations have a stronger legal force than ordinary recommendations.[20]

UN resolutions, especially declarations, often have been the forerunner of treaties. To give a few examples:

- the Universal Declaration of Human Rights (1948) was followed by the two Human Rights Covenants (1966);
- the Declaration of Legal Principles Governing the Activities of States in the Exploration and Use of Outer Space (1963) was followed by a Treaty on Principles Governing the Activities of States in the Exploration and Use of Outer Space, including the Moon and Other Celestial Bodies (1967);
- the Declaration of Principles Governing the Sea-bed and the Ocean Floor, and the Subsoil Thereof, Beyond the Limits of National Jurisdiction (1970) was followed by the 1982 UN Convention on the Law of the Sea;
- the Integrated Programme for Commodities (UNCTAD Res. 93-IV, 1976) led to the Agreement on the Establishment of a Common Fund for Commodities (1980).

Not all UN Declarations have subsequently been followed up by treaties. Sometimes their content turned out to be too controversial, as in the case of the Declaration on the Establishment of a New International Economic Order (1974). In other cases, however, even by themselves they are perceived as legally highly relevant – also in the opinion of the International Court of Justice[21] – and, in whole or in part, as a reflection of the state of the law in certain fields. In this connection reference can be made to the Decolonization Declaration (1960), the Declaration on Permanent Sovereignty over Natural Resources (1962), and to the Declaration on Principles concerning Friendly Relations among States (1970).

'Instant customary law': resolutions which instantly fill a legal vacuum

As early as 1948 Sloan wrote: 'In those areas and on those matters where sovereignty is not vested in a member State, the General Assembly acting as the agent of the international community may assert the right to enter the legal vacuum and take a binding decision'.[22] Indeed, in new areas of international concern – such as the legal regime of outer space and its celestial bodies or the protection of the environment – which demand regulation but where no State practice as yet exists, debates in the United Nations and the resolutions resulting from them, can identify the problems involved and can outline some general principles and guidelines for future regulations and action. In 1965 Bin Cheng developed an interesting theory on so-called 'Instant International Customary Law'. He made special reference to the regime on Outer Space in which general State practice could not have existed in the early 1960s but for which the members of the United Nations, including the United States and the Soviet

Union, unanimously adopted law-promoting General Assembly resolutions. These resolutions proclaimed certain principles for a new common regime as principles of international law. In such cases, resolutions of the General Assembly can serve – in the words of Bin Cheng – 'as midwives for the delivery of nascent rules of international customary law which form within the United Nations'.[23] Such resolutions can indeed generate a new *opinio juris* which under certain strict conditions may grow overnight and may lead instantly to a new rule of customary law.

Permissive resolutions

According to Röling the most important law-creating category of resolutions is that of the so-called 'permissive resolutions': resolutions which do not impose obligations but accord entitlements, even rights to do things which hitherto were not permitted under international law. He pointed out: 'If certain forms of behaviour not usually permissible were recommended, exceptions were created from existing prohibitive provisions. Many States were eager to rely on these exceptions. It was difficult for other States to object to this, now that the action objected to had been recommended by the General Assembly by a majority of more than two-thirds. Action, on the one hand (with an *opinio juris* based on the resolution), and no objection on the other, can very easily lead to recognized customary law'.[24] Thus, legitimization of certain behaviour through UN resolutions may gradually lead to legalisation, through concurrent and widely accepted State practice (customary law) and inclusion in binding legal instruments.

Two examples of this category can be mentioned. Firstly, the 1962 Declaration on Permanent Sovereignty over Natural Resources. This Declaration deviates from the traditional international minimum standard of civilisation governing the treatment of foreign investors, in so far as it formulates certain new principles with respect to nationalization. For example, as far as compensation is concerned, it does not stipulate – in the view of the Assembly's majority – the triple standard ('full, prompt and effective') but 'appropriate' compensation, which would entitle, 'permit', a nationalizing government to take into account not only the damage incurred by foreign investors but also the economic situation of the nationalizing country, including its capacity to pay. This Declaration was supported by a vast majority of States, including many capital exporting and capital importing countries. By reference to the circumstances of adoption the sole arbitrator in the *Texaco vs Libya case* (Award in 1977) concluded that the Declaration on Permanent Sovereignty over Natural Resources expresses the *opinio juris communis* on the nationalization of foreign property under international law.[25] This view may be not entirely indisputable in so far as quite some uncertainty exists over the exact meaning of ambiguous terms as 'appropriate' and 'permanent',[26] nonetheless this Declaration as a whole can be considered as one of the landmark documents in the evolution of modern international economic law.

A second example of permissive resolutions is the set of UN resolutions in which the majority of the General Assembly stated that 'peoples fighting against colonial domination, alien occupation or racist regimes' are doing so in the exercise of their right to self-determination, as provided for in the UN Charter. Some of these resolutions recognize the legitimacy of the struggle of those oppressed peoples to eliminate those regimes 'by all available means, including armed struggle'.[27] Apart from this, such resolutions appeal to member States and international organizations to provide 'moral and material assistance' to national liberation movements, and thus legitimize such support.

These successive resolutions have initiated a legal development by which certain liberation movements and their freedom fighters in territories under colonial domination, foreign occupation or racist regimes are no longer regarded as terrorists, but have acquired a status – be it a very limited one – in international law, especially in the international law of warfare.[28]

Resolutions claiming to impose obligations

This category is more or less the opposite to that of permissive resolutions in the sense that these resolutions do not accord rights, but claim to impose obligations.[29] Examples of this kind include the resolutions relating to the International Development Strategies for the Second and Third UN Development Decades in which governments subscribe to the goals and objectives of the Strategy and firmly resolve to translate them into reality, including the goal that developed countries and 'other countries in a position to do so' (i.e. oil exporting countries with a capital surplus) allot 0.7 per cent of their gross national product to development assistance. The Substantial New Programme of Action for the 1980s for the Least Developed Countries, to which 0.15 per cent of the GNP of the donor countries should be transferred, is another example (UNCTAD, 1981).

It goes without saying that resolutions in which commitments and not entitlements or rights are formulated will not be the most popular ones. They can only lead to the formation of new rules of international law if they are followed up by consistent and sustained State practice.

Programmatory resolutions

As the discussion has led us so far into the domain of international politics, it is pertinent to mention a last category, namely what in French literature is called 'droit programmatoire'. Dupuy has inventively developed the concept of 'programmatory' resolutions.[30] Certain resolutions are prospective in nature, proclaim principles and rules which are new and not yet generally observed, and recommend measures which are not yet instituted.

An example of this category is the Declaration of Principles Governing the Sea-bed and the Ocean Floor (1970), in which the principle of the common heritage of mankind was included as the guiding principle for a new deep sea-bed regime. One can also refer to resolutions relating to ecological questions, for example, the Declaration of the UN Conference on the Human Environment (Stockholm, 1972) as well as 'programmatory' resolutions in the field of development, including the Declaration and Action Programme for the Establishment of a New International Economic Order (1974) and the International Development Strategy for the Third UN Development Decade (1981–1990). Maybe also certain provisions of resolutions in the field of certain socio-economic and cultural human rights have these characteristics. The latter have often been labelled as 'promotional rights'.

The International Court of Justice and the Development of International Law

The International Court of Justice is one of the six principal organs of the United Nations and its Statute forms an integral part of the UN Charter. Nonetheless, the Court has an independent position in the UN system. In this respect it differs, for example, from the General Assembly or the Security Council, whose decisions are those of the Organization as a whole.

The Court passes judgements in contentious cases and gives advisory opinions on questions of law.

Under Article 34 of the Statute 'only States may be parties in cases before the Court'. No other subject of international law has legal standing (*locus standi*) before the Court in contentious proceedings. The Court renders decisions in all 'legal disputes' which States have referred to it. Such decisions are binding, but only for the parties concerned and for each particular case. From 1946 to 1986 the Court rendered 49 judgements.

The advisory capacity of the Court is only available to the General Assembly and the Security Council, and the UN organs and specialized agencies authorized by the General Assembly, but in any case not to States. Unlike judgements, advisory opinions are, in principle, not binding. Since 1946 the Court has provided 18 advisory opinions.

Both judgements and advisory opinions have made an important contribution to the development of public international law and the law of international institutions.

As far as judgements are concerned, this is evidenced in particular by the series of judgements by the Court in cases concerning the law of the sea.[31] In its very first case, the *Corfu Channel Case* (*The United Kingdom vs Albania*, 1949), the Court dealt with the question of a right of innocent passage through international straits and the obligation of a coastal State not to allow its territory to be used for acts contrary to the rights of other States. The principles as developed by the Court in this question were included in the 1958 Convention on the Territorial Sea and the 1982 Convention on the Law of the Sea. In its judgement on *Anglo-Norwegian Fisheries* (1951) the Court laid down basic rules for the limits of national economic jurisdiction and the delimitation of sea areas including (historic) titles to bays and 'archipelagic' waters and the concept of base-lines, which had an impact on the rules formulated in the 1958 Law of the Sea treaties. Thirteen years later and in the wake of numerous claims by coastal States to extend their economic jurisdiction, the Court dealt once again with the issue of the rights of coastal States to an exclusive fishing zone and the traditional fishing rights of other States (*Fisheries Jurisdiction Cases*, 1974). This judgement proved to be very important. The UN Conference on the Law of the Sea elaborated upon it in the 1970s. The contribution of the Court to the development of the modern law of the sea has probably been most significant in its judgements in cases concerning the delimitation of continental shelves. In the *North Sea Continental Shelf Cases* (1969) the Court defined a continental shelf of a State as 'a natural prolongation of its land territory into and under the sea, without encroachment on the natural prolongation of the land territory of the other', and stated that its delimitation was to be effected by agreement in accordance with 'equitable principles'. In the *Continental Shelf* case between Tunisia and Libya (1982) the Court concluded, however, that there was only one continental shelf area, which is common to both States, thereby precluding 'natural prolongation' as a criterion for assessing delimitation. Therefore, the delimitation was effected in accordance with equitable principles, at the same time taking into account all relevant circumstances which characterize the area. In this judgement, the Court elaborated on the concept of equity and the mutual relationship between law and equity. Another interesting aspect of this case was that, upon the request of the parties, the Court also based its judgement on 'new accepted trends' in the Third UN Conference on the Law of the Sea which was then still in the process of drafting a new convention. In its judgements in the cases concerning delimitation of the maritime boundary in the *Gulf of Maine Area* (*Canada vs United States*, 1984) and the *Continental Shelf between Libya and Malta* (1985), (a chamber of) the Court found again that the principle of natural prolongation could not be applied and that the delimitation was to be effected by the application of equitable criteria and by the use of practical methods capable of ensuring an equitable result. In the latter case, the Court stated that the equidistance line was, in principle, the most relevant method to arrive at an equitable result, which could be achieved by provisionally drawing an equidistance line and adjusting it by taking into account a number of circumstances and factors including the configuration and length of the opposite coasts of the parties and the need to avoid 'any excessive disproportion' in the delimitation. Furthermore, the Court dealt in this case with the relation between the continental shelf and the exclusive economic zone, two institutions in the modern law of the sea which are different and distinct but also linked: 'there cannot be an exclusive economic zone without a corresponding continental shelf'. According to the Court, the practice of States showed that the institution of the exclusive economic zone had become a part of customary international law.

The Court also rendered a number of judgements not related to the law of the sea which contributed to the clarification and further development of international law. For example, in the *Barcelona Traction Case* (*Belgium vs Spain*, 1970) the Court developed the concept of obligations *erga omnes*, obligations towards the international community as a whole including respect for human rights and the outlawing of acts of aggression and genocide, as distinct from bilateral obligations between the parties concerned. In the *Nuclear Tests Cases* (*Australia and New Zealand vs France*, 1974), the Court elaborated on the principle of good faith and the legal consequences of unilateral declarations of government authorities, relevant in this case in connection with the statement made by the French President announcing that the nuclear tests by France in 1974 were to be the last atmospheric tests undertaken by the French government. The judgement of the Court in the case *Military and Para-military Activities in and against Nicaragua* (*Nicaragua vs the United States*, 1986) will probably have no decisive impact on the dispute itself. It has, however, been very relevant in appraising the reservations which States have to the Court's jurisdiction and treaties in general as well as in interpreting provisions of the UN Charter and other rules of (customary) international law, notably the prohibition of the threat or use of force against the territorial integrity or political independence of any state and the right of self-defence.

In its advisory opinions the Court has often dealt with the interpretation of treaty provisions and the powers of the various UN organs and specialized agencies. An advisory opinion has, of itself, no binding force. From a strictly legal point of view, it is a far weaker statement of the law than a judgement. They are, however, less related to the particularities of a certain dispute and therefore the Court quite often has greater freedom to deal with more abstract issues and to enter a wider domain of the law. In the opinion of Judge Lachs: 'Advisory opinions offer the Court a much greater potential to develop the law further than do judgements in contentious proceedings: the former, unlike the latter, are not limited to a strict analysis of the facts and submissions that are presented to the Court. An advisory opinion may be broader in scope, focusing on issues indirectly related to the fact pattern, so long as the goal of providing an answer to the question is achieved'.[32]

Several advisory opinions contain innovative elements for the development of public international law and the law of international institutions. For example, the Advisory Opinion of the Court on the *Reservations to the Genocide Convention* (1951) contributed to the development of the law of treaties, especially as far as reservations with respect to multilateral treaties are concerned. The rules laid down in this Opinion of the Court became the basis of the relevant provisions in the Vienna Convention on the Law of Treaties (1969). Also, the Court concluded in its Advisory Opinion on *Reparation for Injuries Suffered in the Service of the United Nations* (1949) that the United Nations itself possesses an objective international legal personality, as a subject of international law, and therefore had the capacity to bring an international claim. In its Advisory Opinion on *Certain Expenses of the United Nations* (1962) the Court dealt with the respective functions and competences of the Security Council and the General Assembly and concluded that the General Assembly had the capacity to establish a UN Peace Keeping Force.

In the Advisory Opinion on *South West Africa/Namibia* (1971), the Court gave interpretations of several key articles of the UN Charter and made very interesting observations on the legal character of certain resolutions of the General Assembly and the Security Council. Upon the basis of these lengthy, more or less preliminary considerations, the Court gave an answer to the question tabled by the Security Council: 'What are the legal consequences for other States of the continued presence of South Africa in South West Africa, notwithstanding Security Council Resolution 276?'

In this way, advisory opinions of the Court serve as a means of securing an authoritative interpretation of the Charter provisions and other rules of international law, as a guide to the various UN organs and specialized agencies in the performance of their functions, and, lastly, as a form of recourse to judgements of administrative tribunals of the UN system by outlining a due process of law.[33]

Conclusions

1. The progressive development and codification of international law can no longer be separated from the United Nations and its specialized agencies. They are indissolubly linked.

    The development of international law has expanded in the last 40 years, probably far beyond the imagination of those who drafted the UN Charter.

2. In the context of the United Nations, an impressive number of multilateral treaties has been concluded. Treaties are of ever-growing importance in international law and have become major instruments of co-operation between States, reflecting the interdependence of States in many fields. Treaty law today can no longer be seen merely as a conservative force in international relations, as an instrument for the maintenance of the *status quo* which solely serves the interests of the developed countries. Apart from being instruments of co-operation between States, treaties have often become instruments of change: for example in the fields of human rights and self-determination of peoples, the law of the sea and the law of treaties itself. Maintaining the *status quo* is, however, sometimes useful as arms control treaties concluded under the auspices of the United Nations show.

3. As was apparent in the first part of this chapter, the multilateral treaty-making process in the UN framework is rather uncoordinated and fragmentary. The International Law Commission, the General Assembly

and its committees and organs, permanent and *ad hoc* bodies, state conferences, and specialized agencies are all involved in this process. A more or less chaotic situation has emerged. Moreover, the process has become very time consuming.

A review of the multilateral treaty-making process was recently included on the agenda of the General Assembly.[34] It is to be hoped that a more uniform procedure will be devised. Another relevant point is that drafting a treaty is one thing, but to secure its ratification and ensure its implementation is another. A number of important multilateral treaties cannot be implemented because the required conditions for their entry into force have not yet been met, as in the case of the Common Fund for Commodities (1980) and the UN Convention on the Law of the Sea (1982).

4. The UN Charter entrusted the General Assembly with special responsibilities in four main fields, which have also evolved as the Organization's main areas of concern:

- the development of friendly relations between States, including measures aimed at strengthening universal peace and security;
- the process of decolonization;
- the promotion of respect for human rights;
- international co-operation for development.

In all these respective fields the General Assembly has an impressive record. The General Assembly and its organs perform this task, firstly, by serving as a 'clearing-house' in tracing the relevant facts; secondly, by acting as a stock-taker of the demands of all member States; thirdly, by providing a world-wide forum for public debate, sometimes referred to as 'parliamentary diplomacy' and 'collective legitimization'; and fourthly, by formulating and recommending new principles and rules of international law, a function which has been characterized as 'quasi-legislative'.[35]

5. UN resolutions, in particular General Assembly resolutions, have played a key role in the progressive development of international law although, of course, not every resolution lends itself to this end. In appraising the legal value of a specific resolution, one has to take into account, as Verwey has suggested,[36] such factors as its contents (is it legally relevant?), its form (the form of a declaration suggests greater value than an ordinary resolution), the wording (is it compulsory or recommendatory, vaguely or concretely formulated?), the voting result (was it adopted unanimously, by consensus, or by a majority – large or small?), and whether States expressed reservations or made interpretative statements (with respect to important paragraphs?).

Furthermore, in this chapter an attempt has been made to classify the legally most relevant resolutions. Eight groups of decreasing legal significance have been identified, ranging from binding decisions addressed to member States to programmatory resolutions. Their legal value may vary

51

widely, but all of them, including the last categories, have had significant effects on the progressive development of international law in the main fields of concern to the United Nations.

6. The formulation and widely-supported acceptance of the universal validity of human rights and self-determination of peoples became incompatible with the maintenance of colonial relations. The ensuing process of decolonization brought about within the United Nations has led to a radical change of the Organization itself.

The newly-independent States have used the United Nations as the central forum for expressing their fundamental objections to the existing international economic order (the Bretton Woods Order), which was established at a time when most of the developing countries did not yet exist as independent States. The new States have consistently tried to expand the powers and activities of the United Nations, including areas which are within the jurisdiction of the GATT and the specialized agencies, such as the IMF and World Bank Group. The UN debate on the development problem and the resolutions resulting from it have substantially contributed to the gradual formation of a normative framework for international social and economic co-operation of States to promote development. As a result, the 'international law of development', or 'droit international du développement' is now seriously discussed.[37]

Of course, the general recognition and consolidation, let alone the subsequent implementation of these principles and rules of international development law may still be far away, yet they have already been shown to have some impact on State practice and the policies of the relevant specialized agencies. No doubt, international economic law is itself developing from a traditional 'international law of co-existence' towards a modern 'international law of co-operation', as Friedmann put it, as far back as 1964.[38]

7. The International Court of Justice has also played an important role in the consolidation and progressive development of international law. Although States are rather reluctant to submit their disputes to judicial settlement by the Court, between 1946 and 1986 the Court has delivered 49 judgements and several of them are widely considered as authoritative interpretations of rules of international law or even serve as a source of international law, for example, in the field of the law of the sea. The same applies to the 18 advisory opinions given by the Court up to 1986. They have, in principle, no binding force of themselves and in this respect they are far weaker statements of the law than a judgement. However, they quite often offer the Court more freedom to deal with more abstract issues, because they are less related to a particular dispute. In this way many advisory opinions contain innovative elements for the development of public international law and the law of international institutions.

8. Law is not static but in a continuous state of flux. One can only assess the

contribution of the United Nations and its specialized agencies to the development of international law, if one considers 'law as a process'. Basically, a process of progress, but all too often also of stagnation and even decline. One has to enter the 'grey zones'[39] between politics, 'soft' law and 'hard' law in order to understand the role that international law could and should play in the fields of development, the maintenance of peace and security, and the promotion of respect for human rights.

Notes

1) William F. Buckley, Jr , *United Nations Journal. A Delegate's Odyssey*, New York, 1977, p. 237.

2) Text of a lecture of Secretary-General Perez de Cuellar, entitled 'Vision and reality: The United Nations at Forty and the Making of International Law', Edinburgh University, 22 January 1985, Press Release *SG/SM/568*, p. 8.

3) Stephen M. Schwebel, 'The Effects of Resolutions of the UN General Assembly on Customary International Law', in: *Proceedings of the American Society of International Law*, 73rd annual meeting, Washington, 1979, p. 302.

4) Mohammed Bedjaoui, *Towards a New International Economic Order*, New York/London, 1979, pp. 133–144.

5) Cf. *Yearbook of the International Law Commission*, 1956, Vol. II, pp. 255–256, paras. 25–26. Similarly, with respect to its draft Convention on the Law of Treaties the ILC observed: 'The Commission's work on the law of treaties constitutes both codification and progressive development of international law in the sense in which those concepts are defined in article 15 of the Commission's Statute, and, as was the case with several previous drafts, it is not practicable to determine into which category each provision falls', *Yearbook of the ILC*, 1966, Vol. II, p. 177, para. 35.

6) An overview of the work of the ILC is contained in: *United Nations, The Work of the International Law Commission*, third edition, New York, 1980.

7) M. El Baradei, Thomas M. Franck, R. Trachtenberg, *The International Law Commission: The Need for a New Direction*, UNITAR, New York, 1981, p. 3.

8) Cf. D.W. Bowett, *The Law of International Institutions*, London, 1982, pp. 140–147; C.W. Jenks, *Social Justice in the Law of Nations, the ILO Impact after Fifty Years*, Oxford, 1970.

9) Cf. B.V.A. Röling, *International Law in an Expanded World*, Amsterdam, 1960, pp. 73–74; L.F. Chen, *State Succession Relating to Unequal Treaties*, Hamden, Conn., 1974.

10) Mohammed Bedjaoui, *op. cit.* note 4, p. 139.

11) Cf. H.G. Schermers, 'International Organizations, Resolutions', in: R. Bernhardt (ed.), *Encyclopaedia of Public International Law*, vol. 5, Amsterdam, 1983, pp. 159–160.

12) G. Abi-Saab, 'The Legal Formulation of a Right to Development (Subject and Content)', in: R.J. Dupuy (ed.), *The Right to Development*, The Hague, 1980, p. 162.

13) W.D. Verwey, 'The Establishment of a New International Economic Order and the Realization of the Right to Development and Welfare', in: *Indian Journal of International Law*, vol. 21, 1981, pp. 26–27.

14) Sadruddin Agha Khan, 'Legal Problems Relating to Refugees and Displaced Persons', in: *Recueil des Cours de l'Académie de Droit International de la Haye*, vol. I, 1976, p. 343.

15) *UNCIO Documents*, 1945, vol. 13, p. 709. The right of auto-interpretation of member States, however, has been maintained. A proposal by the Belgian delegation to grant the General Assembly 'the sovereign competence to interpret the provisions of the Charter' was rejected; cf. *UNCIO Documents*, 1945, vol. 3, p. 339.

16) Cf. H. Reicher, 'The Uniting for Peace Resolution on the Thirtieth Anniversary of its Passage', in: *Columbia Journal of Transnational Law*, vol. 20, 1981, pp. 1–49.

17) Cf. for a critical view, G. Arangio-Ruiz, *The United Nations Declaration on Friendly Relations and the System of the Sources of International Law*, Alphen a/d Rijn, 1979.

18) Cf. Michael Akehurst, 'Custom as a source of international law', in: *British Yearbook of International Law*, vol. 47 (1974–75), pp. 1–21.

19) D.W. Bowett, *op. cit.* note 8, p. 46. Cf. Rosalyn Higgins: '...the body of resolutions, taken as indications of a general customary law, undoubtedly provides a rich source of evidence', in: Rosalyn Higgins, *The Development of International Law through the Political Organs of the United Nations*, London, 1963, p. 5.

20) Cf. O.Y. Asamoah, *The Legal Significance of the Declarations of the General Assembly of the United Nations*, The Hague, 1966.

21) Cf. H. Thierry, 'Les résolutions des organes internationaux dans la jurisprudence de la Cour Internationale de Justice', in: *Recueil des Cours de l'Académie de Droit International de la Haye*, 1980, pp. 393–446.

22) F.B. Sloan, 'The Binding Force of a 'Recommendation' of the General Assembly of the United Nations', in: *British Yearbook of International Law*, vol. 25, 1948, p. 23.

23) Bin Cheng, 'United Nations Resolutions on Outer Space: 'International Customary Law'?', in: *Indian Journal of International Law*, vol. 5, 1965, p. 39.

24) B.V.A. Röling, 'International Law and the Maintenance of Peace', in: *Netherlands Yearbook of International Law*, vol. IV, 1973, p. 23.

25) *Texaco Overseas Oil Company vs Libyan Arab Republic*, Award on the

Merits of an International Arbitral Tribunal, 1977, paras. 84–88, published in: *International Legal Materials*, vol. 17, 1978, pp. 3–37.

26) Cf. W.D. Verwey and N.J. Schrijver, 'The Taking of Foreign Property: A New Legal Perspective?', in: *Netherlands Yearbook of International Law*, vol. XV, 1984, pp. 80–81.

27) W.D. Verwey, 'Decolonization and *Ius ad Bellum*. A Case Study on the Impact of the UN General Assembly on International Law', in: R.J. Akkerman *et. al.*, *Declarations on Principles. A Quest for Universal Peace*, (*Liber Röling*), Alphen a/d Rijn, 1977, pp. 121–140.

28) Cf. Article 1, paragraph 4 of the Protocol Additional to the Geneva Conventions of 12 August 1949, and relating to the protection of victims of international armed conflicts: 'The situations referred to in the preceding paragraphs include armed conflicts in which peoples are fighting against colonial domination and alien occupation and against racist regimes in the exercise of their right of self-determination, as enshrined in the Charter of the United Nations and the Declaration of Principles concerning Friendly Relations and Co-operation among States in accordance with the Charter of the United Nations'.

29) Cf. P.J.G. Kapteyn, *De Verenigde Naties en de Internationale Economische Orde* (The United Nations and the International Economic Order), The Hague 1977, p. 29. Kapteyn uses the term 'mandatory resolutions'. Because of its connotation with Security Council resolutions under Chapter VII, the present author prefers the above term.

30) R.J. Dupuy, 'Declaratory Law and Programmatory Law: From Revolutionary Custom to 'Soft Law'', in: R.J. Akkerman *et. al.*, *op.cit.* note 27, pp. 245–258.

31) Cf. Sir Cl. Humphrey M. Waldock, *The International Court and the Law of the Sea*, Cornelis van Vollenhoven Memorial Lecture, The Hague, 1979.

32) M. Lachs, 'Some Reflections on the Contribution of the International Court of Justice to the Development of International Law', in: *Syracuse Journal of International Law*, vol. 10, 1983, pp. 250–251.

33) Cf. D.W. Bowett, *op.cit.* note 8, pp. 277–282.

34) Cf. K. Wellens, 'Towards a Review of the Multilateral Treaty-making Process', in: *Revue de Droit International*, vol. 64, 1984, no. 1, pp. 50–74 and no. 2, pp. 141–167.

35) Cf. R.A. Falk, 'On the Quasi-legislative Competence of the General Assembly', in: *American Journal of International Law*, vol. 60, 1966, p. 782.

36) W.D. Verwey, *op. cit.* note 13.

37) Cf. O. Schachter, 'The Evolving International Law of Development', in: *Columbia Journal of Transnational Law*, vol. 15, 1976, pp. 1–17; M. Bennouna, *Droit international du développement. Tiers monde et interpretation du droit international*, Paris, 1983; G. Abi-Saab, 'Progressive Development of the Principles and Norms of International Law Relating to the New International Economic Order', UNITAR 1984, *UN Doc.*

A/39/504, Add. 1; M. Bulajic, *Principles of International Development Law*, Dordrecht, 1986; P.J.I.M. de Waart, H.G.M. Denters and P. Peters (eds), *International Law and Development*, Dordrecht.

38) W. Friedmann, *The Changing Structure of International Law*, London, 1964.

39) Cf. G. Abi-Saab, *op. cit.* note 12, and W.D. Verwey, 'The United Nations and the Least Developed Countries: An Exploration in the Grey Zones of International Law', in: J. Makarczyk (ed.), *Essays in International Law in Honour of Judge Manfred Lachs*, The Hague, 1984, p. 531.

5 The Development and Future Role of the International Monetary Fund and the World Bank

H. Onno Ruding*

Introduction

The theme of this chapter is the development and the future role of the Bretton Woods institutions – the International Monetary Fund (IMF) and the World Bank.

It may be useful to begin with a brief description of the history of these institutions, both of which had their origins as specialized agencies of the United Nations. During the past 40 years both IMF and World Bank have continuously adapted their activities to the changing international financial and economic conditions. It is remarkable that the institutional structure of both institutions has been preserved in this adjustment process. This structure in many respects differs fundamentally from that of most other UN institutions. A cautious comparison between the two types of structures will be made in order to account for the differences in performance between the IMF and World Bank on the one hand and UN institutions on the other. This will be followed by comments on some points of criticism made about the IMF and the World Bank, and discussion of some reforms that have been proposed in this context and which

* H. Onno Ruding has been the Minister of Finance in the Dutch government since 1982. In this capacity he is The Netherlands' Governor of the World Bank and the regional development banks. Since 1985 he has been the Chairman of the Interim Committee of the IMF and in 1985/6 he was Chairman of the Group of Ten most industrialized countries. Before his political career he worked for a large commercial bank and was Executive Director of the IMF between 1977 and 1981.

apply to both institutional and policy aspects. In the course of this discussion I hope to make it clear that by and large, I do not support these reforms. Finally, I intend to give a brief indication of my own views on the role of the IMF and the World Bank for the more immediate future.

History and Relationship with the United Nations

The IMF and the World Bank find their origin in the Bretton Woods conference which was held from July 1 to July 22, 1944. With the benefit of hindsight, I believe it can be said that this meeting was one of the most successful of this century and represented a benchmark in international financial and monetary history.

The Bretton Woods conference, officially announced as the United Nations Monetary and Financial Conference, took place in an atmosphere of determination and idealism which was also the fertile soil for the negotiations on the UN charter and the foundation of other so-called specialized agencies of the United Nations, several years later. Actually, a large number of countries came to the conclusion that because of the increasing internationalization of numerous problems of an economic, social and technological nature, individual sovereign states were no longer in a position to cope adequately with these matters. Specialized international organizations, manned and managed by highly trained specialists, were to become the platforms for tackling the various problems. The evolution of these kinds of institutions could in principle have an important favourable effect, namely a depoliticization of international matters. This, it was thought, would lead to a more dispassionate, 'technical' approach to these questions and smooth the path towards solutions.

In 1947 the Bretton Woods institutions and the United Nations signed Agreements which formally laid down that the IMF and the World Bank are specialized agencies of the United Nations. The negotiations on the Agreements with the United Nations took considerable time because of the fear of the IMF and the World Bank that the position of being a specialized agency of the United Nations would subject them to undesirable political control or influence and hurt the Bank's credit rating. As a consequence the Agreements contain special-privilege clauses which ensure the independence of the IMF and World Bank. The Agreements emphasize the need for both institutions to function as independent international organizations because of their special international responsibilities and the terms of their Articles of Agreement. Furthermore, the Agreement not only stresses the limitations to which the Bretton Woods institutions (and the United Nations) are subject in order to safeguard confidential information, but they also limit the right of reciprocal representation, representatives of the United Nations being permitted to attend only meetings of the Board of Governors of the Bank and Fund and being excluded from meetings of Boards of Executive Directors. In addition the

Agreement with the World Bank stipulates that action to be taken on any loan by the Bank 'is a matter to be determined by the independent exercise of the Bank's own judgment' and 'that it would be sound policy for the United Nations to refrain from making recommendations to the Bank with respect to particular loans or with respect to terms or conditions of financing by the Bank'. As a result of the special privilege clauses in the Agreements between the United Nations and the Bretton Woods institutions, the latter are indeed very 'special' specialized UN agencies. Both Bretton Woods institutions have always led a life clearly outside the United Nations' context. Therefore, both Fund and Bank are in fact independent organizations and their statutes make no explicit reference to the United Nations. In day-to-day operations there are few contacts between officials of the Bretton Woods institutions and the United Nations, although naturally there are frequent contacts between the World Bank and UN organizations working in the area of development assistance. In addition, the IMF and the World Bank have a special representative at the United Nations and occasionally all leaders of the specialized UN agencies meet under the chairmanship of the Secretary General.

The memberships of the Bretton Woods institutions and the United Nations show much resemblance. The main difference between them at present is that some communist countries that are members of the United Nations are not members of either the IMF or the World Bank. During the last few years, more communist countries have followed earlier examples (such as Romania) and joined the Fund and the Bank: in 1980 the People's Republic of China joined, followed in 1982 by Hungary, in 1984 by Mozambique and by Poland in 1986. Membership of the United Nations, however, is not a precondition for entering the Fund and the Bank, neither does membership of the United Nations give the right to join the Bretton Woods institutions.

Before discussing certain aspects of the relations between the United Nations and the IMF and the World Bank in more detail, I would first like to give a brief description of the original tasks of the Fund and the Bank and their evolution over the last 40 years.

The IMF: Operations and their Evolution

The IMF was established in 1944 as a reaction to the monetary disorder of the 1930s. The allied countries, including the Soviet Union, drafted a number or rules relating to an orderly post-war international monetary system.

First there was the agreement that IMF member countries would commit themselves to the maintenance of a par value system, thus avoiding competitive devaluations and multiple currency practices. In addition, restrictions on current international payments would gradually be eliminated in order to benefit from the international division of labour. A multilateral and liberal payments system was envisaged. The IMF would have to implement surveillance over member States' compliance with these obligations.

Futhermore, it was one of the main tasks of the IMF to assist member countries confronted with balance of payments problems. The Fund could make available to such countries temporary balance of payments assistance in the form of additional monetary reserves in order to help them avoid the use of restrictions on current payments or a harmful devaluation, on condition that they co-operated with the IMF in order to eliminate the imbalances by way of an adjustment programme. By means of this instrument, both fixed exchange rates and the liberalized current international payments could be established in an increasing number of member countries. Only in case of a fundamental disequilibrium could the exchange rate be adjusted and then only with the permission of the Fund secured in advance.

The present IMF differs in many respects from that which the founders had in mind. Its role has continuously been adapted to changes in the world economy and the international monetary system. The Bretton Woods parity system largely embodied the surveillance role of the IMF until the beginning of the 1970s. In the first years of its existence the Fund had to build up prestige in this area. During the 1960s, the impact of the role of the Fund with respect to the exchange rates of the major currencies was gradually strengthened. The growing balance of payments deficits of the United States, however, put strain on the gold convertibility of the US dollar, which resulted in 1971 in the collapse of the fixed parity system.

Following this turbulent period in monetary history there were several years of uncertainty about the shape of the future exchange rate system. The surveillance role of the Fund was carried out in a vacuum. The current exchange rate system emerged during the 1970s. It was formally confirmed and laid down by the second amendment of the Fund Articles of Agreement in 1976 in which the expression 'a system of stable exchange rates' was replaced by 'a stable system of exchange rates' and new procedures for firm Fund surveillance over members' exchange rate policies were introduced.

Despite these adjustments, the role of the IMF in monitoring the exchange rates of, in particular, the major currencies has hitherto not been very substantial. During the last ten years, the world economy continued to be confronted with, at different times, undesirably high exchange rate variability, which resulted in a growing need for strengthening of Fund surveillance.

The financial role of the Fund has also evolved during the last 40 years. The initial financial impact of Fund activities was relatively small, but at the end of the 1950s, during the Suez crisis and in the course of the 1960s, because of several pound sterling crises, temporary surges in Fund financing activities occurred. During this period there were indications of a growing shortage of international reserves, and in 1969 a new financial role of the Fund emerged: the creation of international reserves through an allocation of Special Drawing Rights (SDR) to the member countries. However, so far, the role of the IMF as a provider of unconditional liquidities has remained of relatively minor importance.

In the years after the first oil crisis the resulting payments imbalances caused concern with respect to the possible introduction of exchange rate depreciations and restrictions on international trade and payments. The IMF reacted by introducing, on a temporary basis, the so-called oil facilities, thus providing additional financial resources. Nevertheless, only a small fraction of the external financing needs of member countries was covered by Fund financing during the mid-1970s. Countries increasingly resorted to borrowing from international commercial banks and from the international capital market for this purpose. Credit-worthy countries apparently found Fund financing relatively unattractive because of the policy conditions attached to it.

The second oil crisis caused even larger and more prolonged balance of payments imbalances than the first one. Especially lower- and middle-income developing countries, with no or insufficient access to the private financial markets, had to call upon the IMF which responded by substantially enlarging the access to its financing and, in addition, started to give more medium-term financing by means of the Extended Fund Facility.

Whereas in earlier years a large part of IMF credit was granted to industrial member countries (for example the United Kingdom), since the late 1970s new Fund credit has gone almost exclusively to developing member countries.

In 1982 a number of middle-income developing countries encountered great difficulties because of their excessive obligations to both official and private creditors. The process of recycling through the international financial markets stagnated, and a large number of countries turned to the IMF, mostly at a too advanced stage of their difficulties. In solving the problems of these indebted developing countries the IMF developed a new role as a catalyst of co-ordinated balance of payments financing. Despite the fact that the Fund provided the countries concerned with large amounts of fresh money, Fund financing was far from adequate to accommodate all financing needs. Therefore, the Fund aimed at mobilizing additional financial resources and restructuring current obligations. The key role of the Fund in solving the international debt problem on a case-by-case basis, consists of an effective surveillance of the implementation of the necessary adjustment policies, in combination with maintaining the required credit flows at an adequate level. In other words: a combination of finance and adjustment.

The role of the Fund in solving the international debt crisis once again confirms that it is indispensable both as a monetary institution and as an international panel for consultation and co-ordination. The events, in many respects turbulent, in the world economy during the last 40 years have, in fact, only strengthened the interest of all Fund member countries in the satisfactory functioning of the IMF.

The Evolution of the Operations of the World Bank

The International Bank for Reconstruction and Development – more commonly called the World Bank – focused its activities during the first decennium of its existence primarily on the reconstruction of post-war Europe. Subsequently, however, its primary objective has shifted to encouraging the development of productive facilities and resources in the developing countries. This objective is carried out through the extension of long-term loans, predominantly for specific projects, which are funded by Bank borrowings in the international capital markets, supplemented by the Bank's own earnings and the paid-in part of members' capital subscriptions. The Bank is owned by the governments of its 150 member countries. It is a particular feature of the Bank's operations that its lending capacity is determined by the size of its capital base, under a statutory maximum gearing ratio of one to one. The Bank acts as a financial intermediary and borrows in the international capital markets against its callable capital guarantees. Currently, the paid-in capital represents only 8 per cent of subscribed capital. The financial leverage derived from Bank borrowings against callable capital guarantees is therefore very substantial. Because of the backing of the industrialized members, substantial annual profits and sound lending for well-designed operations, the Bank has been able to maintain triple A status in the capital markets. The resulting relatively low borrowing costs are passed on to the Bank's borrowers in the form of a corresponding, relatively low lending rate for Bank loans. Besides financial assistance, the Bank extends technical assistance in the form of policy advice in general and project advice in particular. It is the combination of substantial financial resources with the technical know-how of the highly professional World Bank staff which uniquely qualifies the Bank as a development agency.

The development of the world economy over the past 40 years has had an important bearing on the operations of the World Bank, precipitating a transition in its emphasis from reconstruction to development, particularly during its second decennium. The Bank financed mainly infrastructural projects such as roads and harbours in developing countries. The 1970s can be characterized as the decennium of rapid expansion of Bank operations under President McNamara. Whilst external shocks in the monetary and energy fields heavily affected the world economy, new lending by the Bank increased from $2 billion in 1970 to $11.5 billion in 1980. Within the Bank's operations, besides projects in the infrastructural sector, projects emerged which were directed at alleviation of poverty and the provision of basic needs such as employment, housing, education and health services.

The 1980s are burdened with the twin legacy of the 1970s: the debt crisis and protectionism. In reaction to these circumstances the Bank has shown remarkable flexibility in adapting operations to the changing needs of its borrowers. Adjustment has become the central issue and the Bank has responded by increasing its quick-disbursing, policy-based, non-project lending with appropriate meso- and macro-conditionality. With widespread unused production capacity, the revitalization of production has become of primary importance, whilst demand for specific investment loans aimed at enlarging capacity has decreased. The international debt crisis and the increasing importance of non-project lending have brought about a shift in the character of the Bank's conditionality. The conditions attached to specific investment projects are more or less directly related to the project concerned, whereas non-project lending by its nature demands a different conditionality related to the performance of a particular sector or the economy as a whole.

The economic difficulties of recent years in developing countries have also served to sharpen the Bank's long-standing concern with the impact of the wider economic environment on the productivity of investments, on credit worthiness and the ability to attract external capital and hence with the interconnections between project-specific and broader policy issues. As a consequence, in recent years the Bank's management has attached great importance to the so-called policy dialogue between Bank Staff and the borrowing country. Through such a process of constructive dialogue, it is the Bank's goal to achieve consensus with the borrowing government about the conditions which will ensure that a particular operation makes the maximum possible contribution to development. The debt crisis and stagnation of capital flows to developing countries has also made the Bank emphasize its catalytic role. In this connection mention should be made of the Bank's co-financing programme, the extension of partial Bank guarantees on commercial loans and the Bank's co-ordinating role, in particular by means of consultative groups in sub-Saharan Africa.

Bretton Woods and United Nations Institutions Compared

The twin Bretton Woods institutions have, each in its own way, adapted themselves continuously to the changing international environment. Consequently, both institutions, on balance, have functioned actively and well, and have shown practical results. I doubt whether the same can be said of other UN specialized agencies, despite all efforts of staff members and decision-makers. Of course, the Fund and the Bank are not free from criticism, but the main point here is that one cannot reproach the Fund or the Bank for acting inconclusively or passively.

What could be the reason for this difference between the Bretton Woods institutions and the other UN institutions? In trying to make a cautious comparison between them, I note the following four points:

a) First, the Fund and the Bank have substantial financial resources of their own, contrary, for instance, to the United Nations itself, UN Conference on Trade and Development (UNCTAD) and other specialized UN agencies. This enables the Bretton Woods institutions to offer substantial financial support to countries, which enhances their effectiveness in handling problems in their respective policy areas.

b) Secondly, I believe the IMF and the World Bank have high quality staff. Appointment and promotion of staff members is primarily based on personal qualities and not on nationality. On the other hand, UN institutions appoint staff members more on the basis of nationality. This could give more room for political pressures and tends to lead, in practice, to a relatively large number of staff members and to bureaucracy.

c) Thirdly, an important difference between the Bretton Woods institutions and the United Nations lies in the structure of the decision-making process. Within the Fund and the Bank decisions are made by weighted voting. Voting power roughly corresponds with the national capital contributions which ensures that these decisions are in line with relative financial and economic strength. In UN institutions, decision making is based on the principle of one country, one vote. The advantage of the weighted voting principle in accordance with financial responsibility is that decisions are more realistic, practical and are actually put into effect. This principle clearly gives less voting power to the developing countries, although their combined voting power is higher than their share in the capital. However, I think that it is in the interest of these countries that concrete and feasible decisions are taken. The developing countries have no interest in rhetoric and long drawn-out political struggles. It is obvious that avoidance of politicization is much easier to accomplish in technical, financial and economic matters than in purely political affairs. I concur that the latter must be treated in the appropriate body, such as the UN Security Council and the General Assembly. In order to function effectively, specialized agencies, however, should have more interest in a weighted process of decision making.

d) Finally, I would like to point to the more general aspects of the practical and technical functioning of the Bretton Woods institutions. Consultations with management are efficient and aim at effectiveness. There is no publicity attendant to the meetings of the Executive Boards, and hence no posturing. There is no formal right of veto. Most of the decisions are taken with full consensus without divisive voting processes. An example of effectiveness of the current institutional structure of the Fund and the Bank was the meetings of the IMF Interim Committee and the joint IMF-World Bank Development Committee in April 1985 in Washington on the subject of the international debt problem. The consensus between both industrial and developing countries on how to deal with the debt problem was remarkable. The meetings did not carry the burden of the so-called North–South controversy, which in many cases still has a paralysing grip on the UN institutions.

Criticism and Reforms of the IMF and the World Bank

Despite the effective, flexible and on the whole satisfactory functioning of the Fund and the Bank, both institutions are also confronted with criticism. This is probably unavoidable and, in principle, healthy. The main question, however, is whether the criticism of the Fund and the Bank is justified and whether the proposed reforms are desirable. The criticism expressed is directed at both institutional aspects and policy aspects.

Concerning the institutional aspects, it is sometimes felt that the decision-making process within the Fund and the Bank does not serve the interests of the developing countries. It has, therefore, been proposed to enlarge the voting power of developing countries.

It will be obvious from what I have already stated, that I do not share this point of view. The efforts of some developing countries and also of Western critics to draw the Bretton Woods institutions into the North–South controversy is first of all, *not realistic*. Especially in monetary affairs, a simple classification of member countries is not possible. Many classifications, even within the group of developing countries themselves, are possible. For example, countries with balance of payments surpluses and those with deficits, oil producing and non-oil producing countries, middle-income and very poor countries, and debtor and non-debtor countries. In fact the economic and financial interests of countries differ considerably. It is, therefore, not possible to treat the developing countries nor the industrialized countries as homogeneous groups with parallel interests.

Secondly, I consider a change of the voting structure in the Fund and the Bank in favour of developing countries to be *undesirable*. I think that preserving roughly the present voting structure, which is in line with financial responsibilities, is of crucial importance in maintaining effectiveness. After all, it should be borne in mind that this structure has been a major factor in encouraging the industrialized countries to finance the bulk of the activities of the Fund and the Bank. A reform of the voting structure would probably lead to a more reserved attitude on the part of the industrialized countries towards the Fund and the Bank, and may result in a weakening of the financial strength and size of these institutions.

This brings me to a third point: it is *not in the interest* of the developing countries themselves, if the Fund and the Bank should lose the backing of the industrialized countries. With respect to the IMF, the world could lose its only universal monetary institution and all members, including the developing countries, would suffer from that loss. Furthermore, declining support from the industrialized countries would jeopardise the AAA-rating and the funding of the World Bank in the capital markets with direct negative consequences for the developing countries.

A second category of criticism of the Fund and the Bank relates to policy matters. It is, for instance, common knowledge that the IMF is often criticized because of the conditionality it imposes on countries receiving balance of payments assistance. I am convinced, however, that, although some aspects of conditionality in a rare number of concrete cases may be questionable, this conditionality is essential to the effectiveness of the IMF. It is in the interest of each member country, developed and developing alike, that external imbalances be reduced and eliminated. In addition, it is to the benefit of other Fund members that the domestic imbalances of the countries concerned are not transmitted to their own economies. And last but not least, the conditionality encourages member countries to use Fund financing only on a temporary basis. Because of this, the so-called revolving character of the Fund resources can be preserved. This is particularly in the interest of those countries whose currencies are used in Fund financing. They want to be sure that their contributions to the Fund, which remain part of their monetary reserves, are liquid and will thus be available when needed.

Another well-known criticism of the IMF refers to the nature of, rather than the fact of, its conditionality. It is said that the IMF dictates or imposes specific packages of adjustment measures, regardless of the problems of the countries concerned. However, this is obviously not the case. There exists no standard package. The Fund carefully considers the specific circumstances of each country in need of balance-of-payments financing. This is logical because otherwise many of the Fund adjustment programmes would fail and that would not, as already mentioned, be in the interest of those countries, neither would it be in the interest of the other Fund members. Nevertheless, it often appears that the Fund prescription is more or less identical in every case. It should be realized, however, that many countries are often confronted with the same type of imbalances, as for example an inadequate exchange rate policy, a sub-optimal domestic price structure, an excessively large and inefficient government sector and, often related to this, a relatively large government budget deficit and inadequate savings and investment.

Frequently, the Fund conditions are considered to be too harsh. It is true that sometimes they are severe. In many cases, however, countries approach the Fund at a very late stage of their difficulties. Earlier corrective action would have been less severe. If there is bad news, one should not blame the messenger.

Also, there is often criticism of the degree of specification applied in Fund conditionality. In reality, however, the Fund never enters into specific policy decisions to be made by the national authorities. The macro-economic adjustment programme contains generally formulated policy prescriptions, but the specific policy measures are at the discretion of the countries themselves. The Fund may present policy options, but the countries must make their own choice. If a sovereign government decides to give priority to, let us say military expenditure instead of provisions for the poorest inhabitants, one can criticize this, but it is neither correct nor fair to blame the IMF. Although the guidelines for conditionality prescribe that the Fund should, in general, take into account the internal political and social circumstances in formulating the adjustment programmes, the Fund is only indirectly involved in these matters. The background for this is, once again, to be found in the technocratic nature of the IMF. It can only function adequately and effectively if it demonstrates a politically neutral attitude towards member countries with their widely varying political and economic structures.

Criticism has also been raised with respect to the World Bank. As a development finance organization the Bank has drawn fire from both industrialized countries and developing countries. Industrialized countries have sometimes criticized the Bank for emphasizing loan quantity above loan quality and for encouraging the public sector more than the private sector. As to the former there may indeed be indications that the World Bank over-emphasized meeting its yearly lending targets. This practice may indeed have eroded somewhat the policy leverage of the Bank and may have affected negatively the quality of its loans. However, it should be stressed that the Bank has strict standards for project appraisal and that evaluation has shown that its projects have had excellent rates of return (on average 17 per cent). Moreover, this criticism seems to be less valid today in view of the decrease in the lending programme for the fiscal year 1985 for the first time in the Bank's history (Fiscal year (FY) 84: $11.9 bln; FY 85: $11.4 bln). This was mainly because of the situation in developing countries. It is gratifying to note that the Bank has not tried to attain its fiscal year 1985 lending target ($12.6–13 bln) by weakening its conditionality.

As for the contention that the Bank favours the public sector more than the private sector, available empirical evidence does not support this. The great majority of Bank lending has been in support of private sector activities or for activities that even in the United States, would be in the public sector. It has also to be borne in mind that there is often not much scope for lending to the private sector due to the small size of that sector in most developing countries. In many cases developing countries lack basic institutional and physical infrastructure and technical know-how which is almost always supplied by the public sector. Through the government of the borrowing country (Bank loans require a government guarantee by its Statutes) the Bank lends both to the public and private sector. The Bank's affiliate, the International Finance Corporation (IFC), does not need a government guarantee and lends exclusively to the private sector. In its approach to funding individual projects the Bank is essentially 'agnostic' with respect to the question of ownership. Its main concern is with the economic policies followed in the developing countries and the efficient use and allocation of resources.

Not surprisingly, developing countries' criticism has been raised concerning the Bank's conditionality. On the external side the Bank's conditionality relates to an open trading system with realistic exchange rates, and the use of world market prices to reflect real opportunity costs. On the internal side, there is an emphasis on appropriate resource allocation, realistic pricing policies, cost recovery, and the maintenance of sensible fiscal and monetary policies. I need not dwell upon the merits of the Bank's supply-side or market-oriented approach, although I recognize that the market place in developing countries, in some cases, reacts more slowly to a change in relative prices due to developmental bottlenecks. The Bank is aware of this and, as I mentioned earlier, seeks to reach a consensus on the appropriate conditionality with the borrowing country in its policy dialogue.

It goes without saying that financial assistance by the Bank and the Fund does not imply approval of national regimes. In my view, political objections against certain regimes should be channelled through bilateral contacts between countries, or perhaps through the appropriate UN body, but not through the Bretton Woods institutions. By their Statutes, these financial institutions are not allowed to take decisions on political grounds; any other attitude would eventually result in cessation of their activities. Their member countries are sovereign nations and rightly expect these multilateral, global institutions to treat them in a politically neutral way. The problem, of course, is that the political preferences of member countries diverge. That consensus on more technical matters of finance and economics is much easier to accomplish, is shown by daily practice in the IMF and the World Bank. In this connection, I note that in the last few years greater understanding has emerged between industrialized and developing countries on international monetary affairs and development assistance. Once again I would like to refer to the recent meetings of the Interim and Development Committee in this respect.

Conclusion: The Future Roles of the IMF and the World Bank

In my concluding remarks I will try to consider the role of the Bretton Woods institutions during the next few years. In general, I expect the IMF and the World Bank to continue their important role in their respective policy areas. In my view the IMF should preserve its basic role as a monetary and balance of payments institution whereas the World Bank should continue to be a long-term credit institution for development assistance. Despite the fact that an overwhelming proportion of its credit now flows to developing member countries, this state of affairs does not − and should not − make the IMF a development institution. Although close co-operation is essential, the two institutions should be kept separate. A merger of the two would have an adverse impact on their effectiveness.

The IMF should exercise firm surveillance over the policy behaviour of all its member States in a balanced way. I consider it desirable to strengthen this surveillance, both in order to support countries in the follow-up of their adjustment efforts, and with a view to promoting greater exchange rate stability. With better balance of payments equilibrium, the financial role of the Fund could get less emphasis, although the Fund should retain the flexibility to cope with external problems of individual member countries. In this respect I think, in particular, of the important role the Fund will continue to play in resolving the international debt problem.

In handling both the debt problem of the middle-income countries and the structural problems of many poor African and other countries, I expect the World Bank to play a more substantial role in the coming years. In many countries the necessary adjustment policies are underway and there is now a growing need to tackle the structural bottlenecks to development.

The debt problem has led to increased interest in foreign direct investments. Their contribution towards development, in terms of both non-debt creating external finance and transfer of technology and management, is increasingly recognized. The World Bank, which already promoted direct investments by means of the activities of its affiliate, the International Finance Corporation, has acknowledged this potential of direct investments and has played a key role in reaching agreement on the establishment of a Multilateral Investment Guarantee Agency (MIGA). The MIGA aims to improve the investment climate in developing countries by providing foreign investors with financial guarantees against non-commercial risks. At the Annual Meeting in Seoul the Governors of the World Bank approved the MIGA-convention. Since then, the MIGA-convention has already been signed by 50 member countries from both the developing and the industrialized world. The MIGA will make a valuable contribution to fostering the flow of direct investments to developing countries.

The World Bank has also responded recently to the structural problems in African countries by means of the Special Facility for Sub-Saharan Africa. Eligible for financing under this scheme are those IDA-eligible countries in sub-Saharan Africa which have undertaken, or are committed to undertake, an appropriate medium-term programme for policy reform. The Facility, with concessional resources of approximately $1.5 billion for a period of 3 years (FY 86–88), will finance quick-disbursing lending operations with meso- and macro-conditionality in support of structural and sectoral adjustment. Most operations would also be co-financed in part by credits from the International Development Association (IDA), the Bank's soft loan window. I am pleased that the Bank has responded so rapidly to the urgent need for concessional resources in Africa. For the future, given the one-time nature of the Facility and the great need for concessional resources in Africa, it is gratifying to note that agreement has been reached on the substantial eighth replenishment of IDA of about $11.5 – 12 billion. Almost half of this replenishment will be needed to maintain (as a minimum) the existing flow of concessional resources to sub-Saharan Africa during a three-year period (FY 88–90).

In addition to these new World Bank initiatives, the IMF established the Structural Adjustment Facility (SAF). Through this new facility, the IMF will channel, in the coming years, an amount of SDR 3 billion of former Trust Fund resources to the poorest developing countries for additional long-term concessional balance of payments financing. The SAF aims at resolving the structural economic problems of these countries by means of comprehensive adjustment programmes. In preparation of these programmes the IMF and the World Bank together will design so-called joint medium-term policy frameworks. Within these frameworks the IMF and World Bank will finance separately their respective programmes with concessional SAF and IDA resources.

At the Annual Meeting of the Bank and the Fund in Seoul (1985), the United States launched an initiative with regard to the debt strategy. The US initiative, put forward by Secretary Baker, calls for continuation of adjustment policies in developing countries, a continued central role for the IMF, more quick-disbursing structural adjustment lending by the multilateral development banks, in particular the World Bank and, last but not least, increased lending by the private banks. The United States envisages a more substantial role for the World Bank in resolving the debt problem by means of increasing the Bank's policy-based non-project lending in support of the adoption by principal debtors of market-oriented policies for growth. I welcome the US initiative because it might lead to a renewed commitment on the part of the United States towards the multilateral institutions and, at the same time, it acknowledges the important role of the World Bank, because of its lending with appropriate conditionality, in redressing structural problems in developing countries. As far as the World Bank is concerned, I think that the character of the Bank as a development finance organization with its unique combination of substantial financing, policy advice and technical assistance, should be preserved rather than making it into a balance of payments institution. A larger role for the World Bank necessitates, however, an early agreement on a general capital increase of the Bank.

For the future, I am convinced that both the Fund and the Bank will retain their effectiveness. This is in the interest of all member countries and the developing countries in particular. Therefore, I do not expect the Bretton Woods institutions to become the centre of a North–South controversy, although, of course, differences of interests between groups of countries will continue to exist.

I do not envisage a change in the relationship between the IMF and the World Bank on the one hand, and the United Nations and its agencies on the other. Unless, of course, the United Nations itself were to change in the coming years, but this is not very likely. The continuing international financial and economic integration calls for, at least theoretically, a complementary international political integration. The national authorities must become aware of the fact that certain problems require an international approach. Their solution must be found through multilateral co-operation and decision making. The IMF and the World Bank have proved that concrete and pragmatic solutions at multilateral level for international financial problems are possible. It is to be hoped that the United Nations will be inspired by this example.

6 Towards a New International Trade Organization?

Jan Pronk*

In this chapter it is intended to focus on the origins and developments of the two existing international organizations which deal with international trade – the General Agreement on Tariffs and Trade (GATT) and the United Nations Conference on Trade and Development (UNCTAD). An attempt will be made to sketch the experience and structure of these organizations against the background of changes in the international economic environment. In conclusion some options for the future development of these organizations will be considered – options which will depend not only on economic but also on political factors. Also I will analyse how far the option I prefer would be realistic, that is the merger of the two organizations into a new one with a broader mandate than each now has separately.

The GATT: Its Background and Early Years

During the 1940s it was recognized that there was need for a new multilateral economic system consisting of (1) agreed principles, policy aims, as well as rights and obligations of countries, (2) a set of policy instruments to be utilized in a consistent and co-ordinated manner, and (3) some international institutions with

* *Jan Pronk* is Vice-Chairman of the Dutch Labour Party and a Member of Parliament. He was Minister for International Development Co-operation from 1973 to 1977 and a member of the Brandt Commission. Between 1980 and 1986 he was Deputy Secretary-General of UNCTAD. Before his political career he was a university lecturer in development economics, and has published in that field.

specific powers in various areas of international economic policy. The emerging consensus grew from the awareness that it was necessary to prevent a return to the bilateralism and discrimination in international economic policy which had prevailed during the crisis of the 1930s and to establish a new and secure basis for expanding world trade and prosperity after the Second World War.

Elsewhere I have elaborated the set of principles, instruments and institutions upon which agreement had been established.[1] I have argued that this set, basically liberal in economic terms, was inherently consistent. In my view, it was a really new system as compared to the non-system prevailing up to 1940, a sort of 'new international economic order' *avant la lettre*. It did contain some major in-built deficiencies, notably the absence of Southern as well as Eastern countries in its establishment and also the fragility of the commitment of governments to execute domestic economic policies in line with agreed international policies. But for over two decades the newly-created system turned out to be a success: it brought stability, full employment as well as unprecedented high economic growth to the participants in the system.

This was true both for the Bretton Woods institutions dealing with money and finance and for GATT dealing with trade, even though their powers were more limited than originally had been envisaged.[2]

At the first session of the United Nations Economic and Social Council (ECOSOC) in February 1946, the United States introduced a resolution calling for the convening of a United Nations Conference on Trade and Employment with the purpose of drafting a charter for an international trade organization and also to pursue negotiations on tariffs. This resolution was approved unanimously. The charter which was subsequently drafted and discussed at the Havana Conference of 1947–1948 contained commitments in many areas of economic activity: employment, economic reconstruction and development, investment, stabilization of commodity markets, restrictive business practices and commercial policy. It also provided for the establishment of an organization which would exercise an active role in all the areas of the world economy falling within its competence and capable of taking initiatives on issues relating to its broad objectives. The international trade organization, however, did not come into being since the United States, the major economic power, soon announced that it would not ratify the Charter.

Instead it was agreed to draw up a General Agreement on Tariffs and Trade, which would concentrate on tariff negotiations and include only those clauses of the Charter which were considered necessary to protect the value of the tariff concessions. The GATT reflected the principle of a free market with trade taking place at prices set by market forces. As a consequence, the only acceptable commercial policy instrument was the customs tariff, and the object of multilateral negotiations was to enter into commitments with respect to tariff rates. Quantitative restrictions to trade were generally prohibited and could be applied, along with other non-tariff measures, only in specific circumstances. Tariff negotiations were to take place on the basis of reciprocity with the results extended to all contracting parties on an unconditional, most-favoured-nation basis (Art. I) aimed at retaining, at all times, a 'mutual balance of rights and obligations'. Finally, it was decided that the GATT would not include articles involving purely domestic policy.

So the basic principles which were agreed upon were the following: (1) open international markets; (2) a free market mechanism; (3) multilateral commitments; (4) unconditional, most-favoured-nation treatment, and thus non-discrimination; (5) reciprocity and thus balance in the process of negotiations towards a free and open market.

With the failure of the Havana Charter, the GATT constituted the only set of multilateral trade commitments. During the first two decades of its existence, these commitments were consolidated and extended through the phasing out of residual quantitative restrictions, and through negotiations of tariff concessions involving ever more products and countries (through the accession to GATT of new contracting parties).

Gradually certain contradictions between theory and practice began to emerge. It turned out that the tariff-based system could not be applied effectively to trade in agricultural products. Moreover, its extension to other than the original contracting parties gave rise to an unforeseen phenomenon known as 'market disruption', in particular after the massive accession of developing countries. The first concession made to developing countries' interests was to recognize their need to protect infant industries (1955). In addition to this, the developing countries wanted the industrialized contracting parties to take positive measures directed toward development objectives. So, in 1965 part IV of GATT under the title 'Trade and Development', was added as a response to the establishment of UNCTAD in 1964. However, in the 1960s and 1970s it became clear that this achievement did not contain many concrete economic benefits for them.

The UNCTAD: Its Origins and Major Areas of Concern

As mentioned above, one of the built-in deficiencies of the post-war international economic system was the fact that neither the socialist countries of Eastern Europe nor the decolonizing developing countries had had a say in the organization of the system. Of course they could speak out on economic issues in the General Assembly of the United Nations and its Committees, but in these fora discussion only resulted in resolutions, not in negotiations aimed at securing binding decisions to be incorporated in national and international law.

Thus the socialist and the developing countries sought to establish within the framework of the United Nations a negotiating forum on economic issues. The basis would have to be universal: negotiations for the benefit of all countries. The number of developing country member States of the United Nations gradually increased with decolonization and statutory independence. They gave high priority to economic development as a logical next step. In response to this it was decided to call a United Nations Conference on Trade and Development to discuss international economic policies, including trade, related to economic growth and development of the third world. This Conference took place in 1964 in Geneva. The agenda included trade in commodities and manufactures, international money and finance, and development aid as well as other economic relations such as those in the field of shipping.

The UNCTAD Conference produced a set of resolutions containing recommendations linking international economic policies of all countries with growth and structural change in the developing world. There was a consensus that such a link was necessary. This consensus could provide a basis for international negotiations in the years ahead. For this purpose it was decided to turn the Conference into a permanent one, as a subsidiary organ of the UN General Assembly.

So UNCTAD became a negotiating machinery, not an organization such as the UN specialized agencies but – like the GATT – essentially a forum where governments, serviced by a secretariat, negotiate. For more than twenty years hardly a week has passed without one or two parallel negotiations taking place on themes ranging from price levels for individual commodities to rules concerning ocean shipping, criteria for market access, restrictive business practices, international insurance, transfer of technology, aid to poorest countries, export credit guarantee facilities, facilitation of customs regulations, and so on.

One may say that from the outset the basic principles of UNCTAD differed from those embodied in the Bretton Woods-cum-GATT system, which had been dominated by Western countries. UNCTAD, having a more universal character, did lay emphasis on (1) equality for all participating nations, including the poorer developing countries and the countries with a different domestic economic (planning) system, and (2) interdependence between economic sectors such as trade and finance. These two viewpoints made UNCTAD give a higher priority to (3) income transfers from rich to poor, (4) the necessity to create stability in basically unstable (commodity) markets, (5) non-reciprocal preferential action in favour of poorer countries and infant economies, (6) intergovernmental measures to correct the market mechanism where this violated equity, efficiency and stability, (7) as well as longer-term arrangements for international flows of capital, technology and trade.

Within UNCTAD, developing countries made a special effort to unite themselves so as to negotiate effectively and not to be played against each other. On the eve of UNCTAD I they established the Group of 77, which soon had more than 77 developing member States. It was only natural that other negotiating countries established their own negotiating groups. This group system created a new pattern of international negotiation on economic issues. It was quite useful as long as the economic and political differences within the groups were smaller than those between groups, or anyway between most individual countries belonging to different groups.[3]

The Decreasing Role of Tariffs in International Trade

As had been envisaged within GATT, a series of consecutive tariff negotiations were held which were rather successful. On an average, tariffs decreased from above 40 per cent to below ten per cent in about three decades. This exercise received a boost from the strong initial consensus on free trade and was supported by the economic boom during the first twenty years. The same period was also characterized by fixed exchange rates, which by their nature – mutual certainty concerning prices and costs – facilitate mutual tariff concessions.

The decrease in tariffs has changed the potential use of the tariff instrument in international trade. Tariffs are low now and – apart from their still prevailing structure which discourages processing industries – are not the major impediment to trade. And because their present levels are the result of multilateral negotiations they cannot be unilaterally changed – at any rate, not raised – to restore trade imbalances.

In addition to this, four important structural changes in the world economy took place:

- the breakdown in the international monetary system;
- the rise of transnational companies;
- the increasing importance of developing countries in international production and trade;
- the emergence of sub-systems in international trade due to the success of regional economic co-operation and integration.

All these had considerable consequences for the GATT system of principles and policies in international trade.

The collapse of the international monetary system in the early 1970s resulted *inter alia* in a shift from fixed to flexible exchange rates. This made the use of tariff instruments less effective; countries preferred to use more flexible trade policy measures. The lack of discipline in international monetary policy also frequently led to postponement of currency adjustments to restore trade imbalances. The result was permanent currency misalignment in many countries, implying over-valuation and under-valuation of currencies, cost distortions and thus calls for protectionism. These were directed at governments, which increasingly felt that they had to act by intervening in international trade. While originally the international monetary system had been set up on the basis of public responsibility for international monetary balance, its erosion was reflected in increased privatization of international money and capital flows. In return, governments felt compelled to deviate from their original choice in favour of a free and private system of international trade to regularize trade flows. So the original system was more or less turned upside down.

A second major change in the world economy was the rise of transnational companies. Their importance grew rapidly in the 1950s and many of them practically became conglomerates, active not only within one sector – from the stage of primary production to those of processing and of production of end products – but also in different sectors related to each other, including, for instance, the production of substitutes, marketing, transportation and finance. This enabled these companies to steer international trade and finance partly as intra-company phenomena, exploiting cost differentials around the world and setting prices as global oligopolies. They also use intra-firm accounting, restrictive business practices and intercorporate links with transnational banks (which are as independent of monetary authorities as transnational companies are of ministries of finance, industry and trade) in order to avoid the effects of (inter)governmental fiscal, tariff, monetary and exchange rate policies intended to correct the market mechanism. This development has made the Bretton Woods and GATT systems of international finance and trade less effective.

The third major factor was the emergence of developing countries in international production and trade. This implied a shift in comparative advantage away from traditional industrial countries – the original contracting parties – to new entrants on the market. Developing countries entering the market were producing and supplying at lower cost, and countries which were already in the market felt themselves unable either to compete or adapt by shifting to new products. In particular, they found it difficult to handle (non-discriminatory) tariff instruments in their trade with these countries and increasingly resorted to other instruments: non-tariff barriers to trade, which by their nature can be used in a selective manner.

A fourth development was the wide diversification amongst categories of trading partners as well as the success of regional economic co-operation and integration in many parts of the world. This led to exceptions to the universal applicability of the rules and principles of GATT. As a matter of fact, the number of GATT contracting parties has increased from the original 23 to almost 90, including not only developed market economy countries but also newly independent and other developing countries and socialist countries of Eastern Europe. For many, however, the benefits obtained from contracting party status are qualified by special protocols of Accession, by non-participation in specific Agreements or by special arrangements such as the Multi-Fibre Arrangement (MFA). On the other hand, many countries which are not members of GATT benefit from GATT treatment through the exchange of most-favoured-nation treatment under bilateral agreements with the major developed importing countries. One can thus identify a paradox in that while the numerical membership of GATT has increased, it has become less universal in terms of its commitments.

The socialist countries of Eastern Europe have developed a separate framework for trade among themselves: the Council for Mutual Economic Assistance (CMEA), based on co-operation in planning and on specialization derived from the co-operation of material production. Each CMEA country maintains a system of bilateral agreements governing its trade relations with other countries.[4] This gave rise to the question as to how GATT criteria and principles can be applied in trade relations with centrally planned economies. The CMEA countries consider the fact that their trading organizations are given the objective of importing up to the limits provided in their economic plans (limits which are set by the availability of foreign exchange) as an indicator of the non-protective nature of their systems. The developed market economies, on the other hand, have contended that the centrally-planned economy in itself represents a barrier to trade. Socialist countries of Eastern Europe have indeed become contracting parties to GATT, but in practice, they do not enjoy full GATT treatment. In particular, these countries do not benefit from the multilateral non-discriminatory safeguard clause of GATT Article XIX (see below), and still face discriminatory quantitative restrictions against their exports to many GATT countries.

Then there is the third category: the developing countries, the majority of which have become contracting parties to the GATT. However, this does not mean that these countries have been fully integrated. The developing countries' heavy dependence on imports, especially of capital goods and, to a growing extent, on food, combined with a no less heavy dependence, in some cases, on a limited number of primary products for export has resulted in wide variations in their ability to import. Their profiles of tariff protection tend to reflect revenue-raising considerations, their quantitative restrictions are meant to discourage imports of non-essential goods. High tariffs are also maintained to protect infant industries. In short, trade has a different function in their economies. Moreover, the ability of developing countries to import is essentially dependent on the availability of foreign exchange. Foreign exchange can be obtained through exports, direct aid or loans. For most of these countries all three sources offer decreasing possibilities.

Thus, the application of GATT principles to developing countries in general has been difficult. Developing countries consider that they have not been able to obtain adequate trade benefits within the GATT system. They opine that GATT's 'overall balance of mutual rights and obligations' has been unequally distributed between rich and poor. For this reason they find it difficult to accept more commitments in addition to their intent to secure industrialization and economic growth.

China represents a somewhat special case. It is not a member of GATT and it conducts its trade with both market and centrally-planned economies exclusively on the basis of bilateral agreements. These together comprise a separate system.[5]

Bilateral agreements, however, still play an important role in world trade. Most countries which are not contracting parties (many developing countries, China and several socialist countries of Eastern Europe), are linked to the GATT system through bilateral agreements under which they exchange most-favoured-nation treatment with GATT trading partners. The exchange of most-favoured-nation treatment takes place within the framework of special treaties, some of which appear to provide greater security of market access than the GATT itself (for instance, those treaties enabling escape from the 'conditional' application of the Tokyo Round agreements; see below).

Finally there are systems intended to direct international trade flows evolved outside of GATT, such as the UNCTAD code on Restrictive Business Practices, the UNCTAD General Scheme of (Tariff) Preferences in favour of developing countries and, last but not least, the international commodity agreements.

The result of all this is that the GATT cannot be considered as a single agreement applying equally to all contracting parties. It can be described rather as a series of agreements, understandings, protocols, etc., loosely falling within the GATT framework (the 'GATT/MTN system'). Some of these deal with interpretations and elaborations of the GATT articles, others with additional obligations not provided for in the GATT itself, while still others constitute what could be described as 'institutionalized non-compliance' with the rules (not always formally recognized as waivers). In many cases these agreements, understandings, etc., are not subscribed to by all contracting parties. In other cases, some contracting parties have been excluded from benefiting from the advantage of the agreements.

Consequences for GATT: Erosion of Principles

The four developments described above have had important consequences for the system of international trade as agreed at the establishment of GATT. I shall list six consequences, three concerning the erosion of GATT principles and three concerning the GATT system itself.

Firstly, the twin fundamental principles of GATT, unconditional most-favoured-nation treatment and reciprocity, have come under pressure. This was partly due to the emergence of developing countries — asking for non-reciprocity — and planned economies — preferring bilateral agreements without multilateral most-favoured-nation consequences. However, the erosion of these two principles was also due to growing structural imbalances in the trade amongst Western countries themselves which gave rise to new forms of protectionism, on a sector by sector basis. For this purpose tariffs are less suited than non-tariff barriers which can be applied selectively and become widespread. They include safeguard actions, countervailing duties, anti-dumping measures and duties, quantitative restrictions, basic price systems, production and export subsidies and the imposition of voluntary export restraints. The combination of the principles of unconditional most-favoured-nation treatment and reciprocity could not be applied harmoniously in tandem to negotiations on non-tariff barriers as they had been in tariff negotiations, especially because non-tariff measures are meant to be less transparent than tariffs, if they are transparent at all.

Secondly, an erosion of the consensus on safeguards took place. The GATT safeguard clause, Article XIX, permits a contracting party to raise tariffs or impose quantitative restrictions in special circumstances. Safeguard action could only be taken in situations of serious injury, or threat thereof, to a domestic industry as a result of the tariff concessions themselves. The action taken is to be temporary and applied on a MFN basis (thus multilateral and non-discriminatory). Affected countries may withdraw or suspend equivalent concessions or other obligations with respect to the country taking the safeguard action. In theory, withdrawals do not mean a challenge to the legitimacy (in economic terms) of the safeguard action, but are intended merely to restore the balance of advantages.

Soon, however, this agreement faced the strains caused by the competitive success of new trading partners – Japan and an increasing number of developing countries.

New entrants that rapidly increase their share in international trade for a given product benefit from the commitments and obligations accumulated over time through negotiations among the traditional major suppliers. Such a country may succeed in making heavy inroads into the domestic and export markets of the traditional suppliers. If the new entrant is a contracting party in GATT then MFN safeguard action by an importing country would affect the traditional principal suppliers of the product and involve compensation and/or withdrawal of concessions by these partners, or even the threat of retaliation. In order to avoid this, a new approach was devised: the concept of 'market disruption', defined as a situation of damage of domestic industry caused by sharp increases in low-priced imports from a specific source.

This concept greatly facilitated the position of the affected importing country and its traditional suppliers. The existence of the 'damage' was not linked to any contractual obligation as in the case of safeguards under Article XIX; it was not attributed to all imports of the product in question but only to products from a particular source. What was envisaged in the market disruption concept was thus not the type of injurious competition foreseen in Article XIX, nor, on the other hand, did it constitute the type of 'unfair' competition which could be dealt with by the measures permitted under Article VI (providing for the application of countervailing or anti-dumping duties against subsidised or dumped imports, on the condition that such imports carry 'material injury' to the domestic industry). The whole concept thus conflicted with the agreed principle that the free play of market forces and prices competition should be limited by tariff rates only.

The gradual erosion of principles may be illustrated by the Multifibre Arrangement (MFA). The consensus on the non-discriminatory application of safeguards on textile trade broke down in the 1960s and the concept of 'market disruption' (thus originating from a 'particular source') was accepted for the first time in the Short-Term and Long-Term Arrangements regarding International Trade in Cotton Textiles. As a consequence of the ever-increasing number of suppliers, the application of the market disruption concept in its original form became unmanageable. New pseudo-economic concepts were introduced unilaterally, such as the never formally accepted 'disruptive imports' and 'low-cost suppliers' which in turn were supposed to lead to 'cumulative market disruption' necessitating policies of 'globalization'. In fact this meant that rich countries imposed a global quota for textile and clothing imports from developing countries.

Since then countries have sought increasingly to apply MFA concepts in other cases. Proposals have been made for 'selective' (i.e. discriminatory) application of the safeguard clause in GATT Article XIX and later for 'agreed selective safeguards'.

Moreover, the principal restrictive mechanism used under the textile arrangements became the so-called voluntary export restraint, viewed as a positive measure for avoiding market disruption. This measure, which without MFA cover, technically constitutes a breach of GATT Article XI by the exporting country, has been applied with respect to many products outside the textile sector. In the mid-1980s the 'illegal' measure of voluntary export restraints has become the first line of safeguard action in current trade relations and a key trade policy instrument.

A third erosion concerns the 'non-reciprocity' principle underlying trade with developing countries. Part IV of GATT states that 'the developed contracting parties do not expect reciprocity for commitments made by them in trade negotiations to reduce or remove tariffs and other barriers to the trade of less-developed contracting parties'. This clause has to be read in the light of the unconditional most-favoured-nation clause under which the developing countries benefit, as a matter of right, from tariff concessions exchanged among developed countries where the latter are the main suppliers of the products concerned. During the Tokyo Round a number of industrialized countries were unwilling to extend the newly negotiated benefits to all GATT contracting parties on an unconditional MFN basis. As a result, some of the new agreements were applied on what has been termed a 'conditional MFN' basis, which means that developing countries would only benefit if they would accept the overall result of the negotiations or provide some form of reciprocal concessions.

One step further leads to the 'graduation' of developing countries. In the same manner that the concept of market disruption led to the establishment of a discriminatory regime largely directed against developing countries, another new concept, graduation, is leading to the undermining of the benefits of preferential treatment in their favour.

The principle of generalized non-discriminatory tariff preferences in favour of developing countries was accepted by the international community in UNCTAD in the late 1960s. The preference schemes applied in the 1970s contained a variety of safeguard mechanisms for limiting the extent to which a given country could benefit from preferential access with respect to any particular product. However, during the Tokyo Round, industrialized countries claimed that as developing countries' economies became more competitive, tariff preferences should be gradually withdrawn. While it was agreed that the General Schemes of (Tariff and Trade) Preferences (GSP) would be recognized as compatible with GATT (the 'enabling clause'), developing countries had to accept that they would progressively participate more fully in the GATT framework and obligations: the 'graduation clause'.

Graduation has been justified as a means of protection against damage from imports from more advanced developing countries and of providing a better opportunity for the least developed among them. Both objectives could be met by a non-discriminatory safeguard clause combined with positive action in favour of the least developed countries. Instead, another route has been chosen: industrialized countries, in particular the United States, increasingly stated that preferential or more favourable treatment of developing countries could be withdrawn unilaterally, without consultation, and/or that the maintenance of such treatment could be made conditional upon the acceptance of new additional obligations by developing countries (for instance in the field of international services). Moreover, concrete positive trade action in favour of the least developed countries has so far not been launched.

Consequences for GATT: Breakdown of the System

The erosion of GATT principles has substantially affected the GATT system. GATT can hardly now be described as a universal agreement based on a common set of principles. The trade agreements that are negotiated within GATT, though legally binding, are only loosely related to the original conception laid down in the Havana Charter. The once universal system has become compartmentalized in at least three different ways. Firstly, sectorialization of obligations took place. Already in the early years of GATT the agricultural sector was, in effect, removed from the General Agreement but a number of waivers and exceptions permitting countries to impose restrictions on agricultural trade and to introduce variable levies and subsidies. However, exceptions created new exceptions and other sectors followed. I have already mentioned the special situation of the textile sector. Shipbuilding, the automobile sector and the civil aircraft sector are heading the same direction. In the steel sector a subsystem based on minimum prices has evolved. Trade practices in consumer electronics no longer seem to be based on multilateral agreement. Increasingly new concepts are developed to justify a separate legal framework which tends toward some form of managed trade. Subsidies are given almost free rein in one sector while they are hardly tolerated in others. Minimum import prices are considered as the appropriate trade policy instrument in one sector, voluntary export restraints in another, and minimum export prices in a third.

This sectorialization gave rise to bilateralism. Countries became less interested in multilateral agreements but preferred bilateral talks, either between individual countries or country groups. Such a preference was shown by stronger countries but also by some weaker countries, which feel victimized by the erosion of the principles of the multilateral system and as a result increasingly opt for bilateral (and regional) instead of multilateral trade arrangements. Some countries went even further than this; observing that the effectiveness of the multilateral system had become weak, they were not deterred from taking unilateral action. Traditional examples were unilateral decisions to heighten protectionist barriers by applying new non-tariff measures and by increasing investment and export subsidies. The multilateral system had been established, in particular, to combat such unilateral trade action, originally with success. However, these measures are now being applied again and complemented by new, more sophisticated examples, such as:

- the unilateral removal of preferences which had been granted as a result of a multilateral consultation;
- one step farther: the unilateral imposition on preference-receiving countries of concessions to preference-giving countries in order to keep these preferences;
- even more cynically: the unilateral imposition on trade partners of such concessions in order to remove trade restrictions which at an earlier stage had been imposed unilaterally.

Increasingly also the mere threat to apply unilateral action seems to be effective. There is a widespread current tendency to try to impose discipline on others whilst retaining a free hand for oneself.

All such developments – erosion of multilaterally agreed principles, sectorialization, bilateralism, unilateralism in trade policy making and harassment of trading partners – have been influenced by the multilateral system being limited to international trade only, with no co-ordination of domestic economic policies (e.g. industrial policy). During the second half of the post-war period international trade agreements have tended to reflect the domestic laws and practices of the major trading countries rather than vice versa. International trade and trade agencies, rather than setting the economic limits for national economic policy – together with international money and finance agencies, as had been the intention at Bretton Woods and Havana – have gradually become no more than simply the derivative of domestic policies. Probably neither of the two approaches will ever work in their purest forms. But in order to have a system which functions well there should be a balanced multilateral agreement on principles and policy instruments with regard to both international and national economic policies.

Some degree of policy co-ordination and interference in markets is required in order to correct and support the market mechanism, when necessary, in order to maintain a balance in flows of capital and trade. Such management should not take place unilaterally because this would breach principles of equity, provoke retaliation and thus again endanger the balance. Nor should it be one-sided, for instance in trade only, without taking proper account of finance, or in international economic relations only without taking proper account of domestic economies, or vice versa. This too, would run the risk of leading to more, rather than less imbalance, which is what happened in the 1980s.

Developments within UNCTAD and New Areas of Concern for both GATT and UNCTAD

Not only GATT but also UNCTAD has changed its character. It is clear from what has been said above about the origins of UNCTAD that from the very beginning financial and monetary questions, as well as specific issues related to technology and shipping for instance, were on its agenda. However, one major development facing UNCTAD has been the increasing unwillingness of the Western countries to discuss financial and monetary issues – including development aid as well as debts – within UNCTAD. This was reflected in efforts to weaken UNCTAD's original mandate, by the means of disputing agendas, refusing to participate in discussions on subjects which were also discussed by other organizations and, on several occasions, even by exercising an empty-chair policy.[4]

The trade area itself is vast and in the early years, therefore, UNCTAD's activities only rarely overlapped those of GATT. This was particularly due to UNCTAD's concentration on trade in commodities, while GATT dealt mainly with trade in manufactures which involved more tariff barriers than primary products. In the 1960s, under UNCTAD's aegis, a number of individual commodity agreements was concluded in order to stabilize prices through international buffer stocks. When this approach turned out to be less successful than had been expected – the number of commodities brought under such a regime was small and the size of the buffer stocks was often not adequate to keep price fluctuations within the agreed limits – a new approach was sought: the Integrated Programme for Commodities grouped 18 commodities to be negotiated together in one package and aimed not only at price stabilization but also at export revenue stabilization and increases, and at improvements of supply and demand conditions (quality, processing, marketing, substitution and so on). This new approach resulted in an international agreement in 1980 to adopt the Integrated Programme and to establish a Common Fund to finance it.[6] However, it has yet to come into effect because the required minimum number of countries ratifying the agreement has not yet been reached. (As a matter of fact, rendering the Fund operational is at present in the hands of either the USSR or the United States, neither of which have yet ratified the agreement.) At the same time the number of operational individual commodity agreements has decreased, partly because of the prevailing tendency against market interference, partly because of disappointment with the case-by-case approach adopted so far.

A second major trade policy area in which UNCTAD has been active is the establishment of General Schemes of (Trade and Tariff) Preferences (GSP) in favour of developing countries. Such schemes did follow the political agreement reached at the Geneva Conference of UNCTAD (UNCTAD I, 1964) which provided for non-reciprocal preferential action in favour of poorer countries and infant industries in developing economies. Many industrialized countries including the United States and Japan as well as the EEC, did establish such schemes. During the GATT Tokyo Round it was agreed that the GSP would be considered as compatible with the General Agreement ('the enabling clause'). However, since then the benefits derived by developing countries from these schemes have turned out to be rather limited: general tariff reductions eroded part of these benefits and preference-giving countries introduced more and more ceilings, exceptions, and less transparent bureaucratic rules for their implementation. Recently the further development of the schemes has been overshadowed by the graduation issue mentioned above.

A third subject in the field of trade discussed by UNCTAD was the trade relations between countries belonging to different social and economic systems. In practice this meant trade between socialist countries of Eastern Europe, which had planned economies oriented towards balancing imports and exports with each of their individual trade partners, and developing countries, most of which were oriented to the world market as a whole but which had structural foreign exchange constraints to trade. East–South trade has increased considerably, but it is problematic to compare its growth with that of other trade flows since the original level was very modest indeed. However, the instrument of longer-term bilateral trade arrangements, combining the preference of Eastern European countries for bilateral equilibria and that of developing countries for longer-term guaranteed market access, has contributed much to the increase in trade amongst them. UNCTAD has, no doubt, played an important role in the further development of such arrangements.

In the 1980s three new areas of international trade have been given much attention within UNCTAD. The first was trade between developing countries themselves in the framework of a programme for Economic Co-operation between Developing Countries (ECDC). The main instrument discussed to further this trade was a General Scheme of Trade (including tariff) Preferences amongst developing countries. Since 1979, when developing countries decided for the first time to make a special effort in this field, not much has happened. Despite many reaffirmations at the political level of the necessity for such a scheme, concrete negotiations have not yet begun. This delay is partially due to objections raised by other countries against developing countries negotiating a programme for co-operation exclusively amongst themselves within a universal UN framework. However, growing economic differentiation amongst developing countries has not facilitated the talks either.

The second new area concerns the least developed countries. This special category of countries has been officially accepted by member states of the United

Nations as the result of UNCTAD's activities since its inception. Other countries undertook a commitment to make a special effort to help the least developed countries not only by means of development aid but also in the field of trade, but it took a long time for this commitment to be translated into action.[7] However, in 1985 the European Community declared that it would extend the STABEX scheme of the Lomé Convention – designed to compensate the ACP developing countries for specific decreases in their commodity export revenues – to all least developed countries. It is a first step and only a small one. But there are indications that developed countries will be more and more willing to implement special programmes for the least developed countries. So far, such action has been modest and has not been accompanied by a decrease in assistance to other developing countries. But statements made on behalf of industrialized countries express an inclination towards trading-off preferential treatment of the least developed countries against more advanced developing ones.

Thirdly, UNCTAD was given an official mandate to discuss protectionism in international trade. This mandate resulted in annual surveys of protectionism in relation to structural change and adjustment in international trade. These have led to several resolutions including one passed at the Sixth Conference of UNCTAD (Belgrade, 1983). This resolution can even be interpreted as one of the strongest commitments made by the international community to put a standstill to protectionist measures and to engage in a rollback. UNCTAD so far has not been allowed to become involved in analysis and negotiations concerning protectionism in individual sectors. Instead it has focused on studies of the protectionist policies of individual countries. It has developed a data bank on non-tariff measures which could provide important information for negotiations in this field, including for instance, those under the auspices of GATT.[8]

In addition to the three areas of trade policy on which UNCTAD had concentrated from the very start (commodities, schemes of preference and East-South trade) and those to which attention was turned later (ECDC, least developed countries and protectionism), three areas of trade policy are emerging which in the coming decade will undoubtedly receive a great deal of attention from both UNCTAD and GATT. These are (1) the relation between finance and trade, (2) trade in services and (3) the consequence of the new technology revolution for international production and trade.

The first area of policy, the relation between finance and trade, is quite obviously an area which requires much attention. The interdependence between the two is clear. The import capacity of countries not only depends on their export revenues but also their debt service payments, on international interest rates, on the availability of export credits and longer-term development finance, and on exchange rate policies. In particular, the debt crisis and the global recession of the early 1980s have made it clear that trade policy cannot be isolated from international finance and monetary policy.[9] But what analytically seems to be self-evident, has not yet been accepted as a basis for international economic policy formulation. International secretariats – including those of

UNCTAD, GATT and the World Bank – have, time and again, highlighted the necessity for parallel action, but intergovernmental response has so far been reluctant. However, the renewed attention given to economic growth rather than adjustment may turn the tide.

The second new policy area is trade in services: banking, insurance, communications, trans-border data flows. These sectors are becoming more and more important both as a consequence of economic development in industrial countries towards a post-industrial society and because of the emergence of the global market, world-wide, without geographical boundaries. Investment, production and trade in goods are increasingly determined by companies with a strong basis in service sectors. Industrialized countries claim the necessity of liberalization of international trade in services by bringing these sectors into the GATT framework. Developing countries fearing that this would mean that their economies would be brought under new foreign dominance by foreign banks and foreign economic consultancy companies before they could build up their own enterprises in these sectors, claim the validity of an infant economy argument for the sectors concerned. They would not wish to remain permanently net importers of services and high technology. They also point to the necessity of implementing GATT rules already agreed in sectors for which they are applicable (agriculture and industry) before bringing new sectors under the same regime. In the longer run it would be in the general interest to establish a regime on the basis of multilateral consensus. Unilateral action, either economically unjustified protection or arbitrary retaliation would create a chaotic situation in 'modern' complex service sectors which, perhaps even more than 'traditional' goods and commodities, would require uniform, transparent and fair rules and standards in production and trade.[10]

The new technological revolution has fundamentally changed production functions and cost relations. The comparative advantages of labour surplus countries are decreasing, while countries where labour costs are high have regained competitive strength due to revolutionary changes in production techniques. Transnational enterprises have maximum information about characteristics of the global market and can easily redeploy resources throughout the world. This is the third and perhaps the major challenge to the trade agenda in the years ahead.[11]

Options for the Future

GATT has changed, UNCTAD has changed, times have changed. The economic situation in the 1980s is quite different from that at the time of the establishment of GATT 40 years ago. It also differs from the one prevailing 20 years ago when UNCTAD was established. Structural change in the world economy, the rise of the third world, technological progress, the emergence of the global market and of transnational companies have changed the picture drastically. To a certain extent changes in GATT and UNCTAD, in terms of both their agendas as well as the policy criteria adhered to, are the result of efforts made by governments to adjust economic policies to structural changes. Such adjustments, which are still taking place, were mostly *ad hoc* rather than based on an integrated view regarding the desirable direction of structural change. That is why both organizations are presently running behind economic developments instead of trying to anticipate, to guide, let alone to lead.

The mid-1980s offers a new opportunity to do so. Economic change and uncertainty have given rise to a climate of political and ideological transition. Economic negotiations, including those between North and South, are at a stalemate. However, there is increasing willingness to do business again, be it on the terms of the economically more powerful countries. Countries weakened by the debt crisis, by stagnation in growth figures and by unemployment, and which are threatened by recurrent recessions, at present seem to give in more easily to demands by stronger countries than they did in the second half of the 1970s. The latter favour a return to a more pure ideology, claiming the necessity of strong market discipline with utmost restraint from market intervention. Multilateral agencies which stood for more equal market access and more equal distribution of wealth and welfare, to be achieved by such interventionist policies, are nowadays heavily criticized. This is truer for the universal social and economic UN agencies, including UNCTAD, than for agencies such as GATT, the IBRD and the IMF, which do not have universal membership or whose decision-making procedures reflect economic power rather than 'one country, one vote' procedures. However, the latter are now also being criticized.

This situation of economic and political transition should be used by GATT and UNCTAD to decide on their future roles. Both organizations face various options.

GATT may finally turn out to be wholly unable to guide inter-governmental policy-making in trade and related areas. This would mean that governments increasingly resort to bilateral and unilateral action and harassment. Trade would cease to have the potential of strengthening and spreading economic recovery and of boosting economic growth. Instead, limits to trade would turn an economic recession into a lasting crisis. The result would be a far from transparent, badly co-ordinated and rather chaotic mixture of inward-looking bureaucratic national economic policies, paralysing international action, let alone co-operation.

The second option for GATT would be to revert to a full application of the original rules and principles. This would necessarily involve the restoration of the tariff as the basic instrument of trade policy and the acceptance of price competition in a free market. It would require the elimination of all illegal non-tariff measures − a reversal of the present trend towards the imposition of export restraints. Moreover, such an approach would require that the economic criteria justifying resort to safeguard action be subject to multilateral approval and surveillance.[12]

The third option would be for the international trading community to decide that a return to a tariff-based system is unrealistic and to address itself to new rules and procedures. These should result in a sort of multilateral management of trade ensuring equity amongst the trading partners. New agreements should be drawn up which would prohibit discrimination against any particular group of countries and provide for measures ensuring greater market access for developing countries. To be anything more than mere protectionist devices, safeguard and similar arrangements would have to include commitments to positive structural adjustment policies as well as measures to increase the share of developing countries' trade of the products concerned.

It is difficult to foresee which option is the most probable one. In 1986 in Punta del Este a new GATT round of trade negotiations was launched. This seems to reflect an increasing awareness that important structural changes in international trade practice are due in order to sustain world economic recovery. A prominent role in these negotiations has been given to agriculture and services. Moreover, during this round the functioning of the GATT system will be reviewed explicitly with the purpose of, amongst other objectives, enhancing surveillance and achieving greater coherence between trade and finance. This could be the beginning of a new GATT: the third option.

Originally, developing countries were rather reluctant to enter the current rounds of tariff negotiations, because they had benefited less from the previous round than the industrialized countries. Moreover, the recent positions taken by the latter do not augur well. Commitments to a standstill and rollback of protectionism are not being implemented. On the contrary, since Punta del Este new protectionist measures have been introduced. There is no tendency to renounce safeguards protecting obsolete industries. Despite the wordings of the Punta del Este declaration there is a risk that new trade negotiations will concentrate on demands by rich countries upon developing countries to open up their markets rather than the rich countries providing greater access to their own markets. Moreover, despite the launching of the new multilateral round, disputes between major trading partners (EC, USA and Japan) continue to be dealt with bilaterally.

The new round could well be GATT's final chance. If negotiations fail and GATT is not be to renewed, some countries might choose a fourth option: reaching new agreements within a selected group of countries only, based upon a strict adherence to the original rules and principles plus additional regimes for new sectors. This combination of options 2 and 3, but only applicable to more prosperous and free market oriented countries, has been labelled 'GATT plus'.[13] For countries not in a position to participate it would undoubtedly result in less access to markets, and thus in 'GATT minus'.

UNCTAD also faces several options. The first one is the same as for GATT: a chaotic situation in the field of international trade and increasing irrelevance for the organization. The second option is to concentrate even more than hitherto on serving the third world directly as a secretariat for the strengthening of economic co-operation amongst developing countries and assisting these countries in their negotiations with others. It is an option which deserves serious consideration. Third world policy-makers lack confidence in their economic self, do not make adequate use of their bargaining power, let themselves be played-off against each other on the basis of short-term considerations, and are not backed-up enough by expertise. But it is doubtful whether this option is politically feasible: unity and co-operation amongst third world countries should have been strengthened ten years ago when the international economic and political situation was much more conducive to this. Moreover, any effort to do so within the framework of the United Nations seems at the risk of being vetoed by other countries on the grounds that UNCTAD should benefit all countries rather than exclusively one group.

Another option for UNCTAD is to wage a battle to regain lost territory and to become fully competent in all matters of international economic policy with consequences for development. Such a battle would be justified. UNCTAD's original mandate has been wide, as agreed by the whole intergovernmental community. Furthermore, structural change which has taken place in the world economy would, in the 1980s even more than in the 1960s, necessitate an integrated approach to development problems. But, justified though it might be, the battle would be lost from its very beginning. The period of benevolence towards the developing countries is over. Rich countries are simply not willing to negotiate on terms less favourable to them than those prevailing in organizations which they can dominate.

This brings me to the last option. UNCTAD could try to influence and catalyse negotiations taking place elsewhere (including negotiations within GATT) on issues for which it does not have exclusive competence. It could do so by assisting developing countries in these negotiations, by researching priority problems of development, publishing timely, high quality studies, challenging vested interests and conventional wisdom, coming forward with alternative recommendations and influencing the negotiating agenda. At the same time, UNCTAD could reinforce its activities in areas such as commodities, for which its competence is not disputed. This option would have the virtue of being both politically realistic and philosophically ambitious.

Again it is difficult to prophesy the direction. However, I am afraid that present attitudes of governments towards UNCTAD — the renewed willingness to do business with each other, but on a no-nonsense basis, preferably outside the United Nations — make the first option (irrelevance) the most likely one for this organization. The Seventh Conference of UNCTAD (Geneva, 1987) took place on the basis of an agenda that was much the same as that of the previous Conference which was an outright failure. Although UNCTAD VII was slightly more promising, it did not provide a breakthrough. Discussions within UNCTAD still reflect more the issues and approaches of the 1970s than the new structural developments in the world economy.

A New International Trade and Development Organization?

Personally I favour the third option for GATT: re-establishing an effective multilateral framework for intergovernmental trade policy making: the multilateral management of trade based on the consensus to strive for an optimum combination of economic freedom, efficiency, stability and equality. I also favour the last option for UNCTAD; that is, dealing with a wide, rather than limited range of issues in an integrated manner, with more orientation towards getting it right than being right. However, I have already indicated that the least desirable (first) options for the two organizations are the most probable ones.

I dare say that any isolated effort to improve either of the two organizations, both as a forum for negotiation and as an institutionalized set of principles and rules, would not work. That is why I would like to go one step further. A big step, not so much in the interest of GATT or UNCTAD but in that of the international community. By choosing the preferred options the two organizations would become more relevant, influential and effective than they are at present, but they would still be reacting to developments, rather than anticipating them. Why not merge the two into one new, strong International Trade Organization?

In the past UNCTAD and GATT overlapped each other's activities much less than many people had assumed. The foregoing description of their activities may serve to illustrate this. However, they are bound to enter the same territory if they want to regain relevance by addressing priority issues concerning trade, growth and development. Structural change in the world economy, as indicated above, and the intensifying interdependence both between countries and between economic sectors will undoubtedly result in a convergence of the main areas of interest for these two organizations.

This would not in itself be a reason for merging. Convergence of areas of interest does not necessarily imply convergence of approaches to the subjects concerned. The ideologies may still not be the same because of the different mandates, and the political choices and recommendations may also differ. As long as there is inequality in access to negotiating tables, unequal political power, this would not be harmful. On the contrary having two, albeit conflicting, approaches would serve a sound political purpose because those with fewer rights at the negotiating table could increase their bargaining power by resorting to alternative analysis, approaches and recommendations.

Would it not be preferable, however, to tackle the root of the problem right away by establishing more equality in decision-making power? Would it not be better to negotiate on an equal footing in a true multilateral framework on the basis of a new consensus between all partners with regard to the basic principles of economic policy, the real content and weight to be given to policy aims, the applicability of trade policy instruments and – last but not least – the rules to be applied in negotiations and policy implementation? How long can the international community afford not to establish such consensus?

Governments might well use the opportunity provided by the economic, political and ideological transitions which we witness today to opt also for institutional change. A new, really global and multilateral institution could help them face the challenge of a new era, when international markets, in terms of supply and demand conditions, will be very different from now. Such a new institution should not simply be the sum of UNCTAD and GATT. It should be different, especially in the following respects.

Firstly, it should not deal solely with trade. Events during the last 15 years or so have shown the futility of attempts to deal with trade in isolation. Interdependence between trade and finance requires reform in international money and finance parallel to that in trade. Matters concerning international money and finance with direct consequences for trade should not be excluded from discussion in a new organization. This should also apply to some other areas of international economic policy (such as flows of technology and the activities of transnational companies).

Secondly, it should not deal with international economic policies without at the same time discussing domestic economic policies both in developed and in developing countries. Since the latter determine the former, rather than – as in the past – the other way round, not to discuss investment, production and employment when discussing finance and trade has become ever less credible. In this sense, a return to the original idea of an international organization for trade and employment could be advocated. Discussing domestic policies with a view to co-ordinating them would facilitate the implementation of longer-term structural change policies rather than short-run adjustments only.

Thirdly, governments should be willing to discuss all this not only amongst themselves but also with representatives of the private sector: (transnational) enterprises and labour unions. Governments, whether inclined to more market intervention or not, now have fewer opportunities to influence market processes than in the past, because of the intensified interdependencies of the global market. That is why they should refrain from unilateral action and should try to co-ordinate with other governments and with other actors in the market. Perhaps in some specific, well-defined sectors of policy making within a new organization the International Labour Organization tripartite structure could be applied.

Fourthly and finally, it should be really universal, with equal rights and obligations for all countries. Decision-making procedures within such a new organization could reflect differences in economic strength. Rules and criteria would have to take into account differences in the level of economic development. Some of them could be the same as those agreed in 1947, some undoubtedly would have to be different. But whatever criteria and rules were devised, once adopted their implementation and translation into obligations at the national level should be ensured.

Already in 1979 the Brandt Commission (referring to previous suggestions) recommended that an 'international trade organization incorporating both GATT and UNCTAD is the objective towards which the international community should work'.[14] However, as has been the fate of many other recommendations by the Brandt Commission, this has not been taken up in any intergovernmental forum. In this paper I have gone one step further, by pleading for an international organization dealing with trade and – domestic as well as international – economic development policies related to trade.

This is necessary from an economic point of view. Is it politically realistic? In 1985 the United Nations celebrated its 40th Anniversary. It did so in a climate of growing criticism. Much of this criticism was ill addressed because it was more the governments than the United Nations as an institution, which had failed to live up to expectations concerning international co-operation. However, change in the institution itself is also due. Initiatives to restructure that part of the United Nations dealing with economic policy co-ordination would perhaps have a greater chance than initiatives concerning the purely political aspects of the organization.

Recently, an interesting proposal was made by a former Inspector of the United Nations, Maurice Bertrand, who advocated *inter alia* the establishment of an Economic Security Council within the Organization.[15] Though the relationship between such a Council and the intergovernmental bodies of UNCTAD and GATT were not spelt out in detail in his report, it is clear that his proposal has the merit not only of reflecting the increased interdependence between economic sectors but also of introducing more effective procedures for intergovernmental consultation. It could even facilitate merger of agencies and fora at a level below that of such a Council.

Anyway, whether more far-reaching proposals concerning a reform of the United Nations, such as that made by Mr Bertrand, were acceptable or not, a merger of GATT and UNCTAD into a new UN International Trade and Development Organization would have many merits. It would enable these organizations to break through the vicious circle of inadequate rules and criteria and lack of political will to change them. It would contribute to more effective international economic policy making. It would also enhance the credibility of the United Nations as a real multilateral organization, where the effective implementation of rules and the outcome of negotiations, once agreed, would matter as much as the negotiation of the wording concerned.

Notes

1) J.P. Pronk, 'The New International Economic Order: A second look' in: John Langmore and David Peetz (eds), *Wealth, Poverty and Survival*, George Allen and Unwin, London, 1983.

2) The following description of developments within GATT relies heavily on *UNCTAD Document* TD/B/913, 'Multilateral Trade Negotiations', 1982.

3) See for an elaborate recent account of the evolution of UNCTAD, *The History of UNCTAD 1964–1984*, United Nations, New York, 1985 (UN

Publication Sales No. E.85.II.D.6); Michael Zammit Cutajar (ed.), *UNCTAD and the South–North Dialogue The First Twenty Years. Essays in Memory of W. Malinowski*, Pergamon Press, Oxford, 1985.

4) See O. Tischenko, 'Trade Policies of the USSR and other Socialist Countries of Eastern Europe: Modalities and Mechanisms', *UNCTAD Document* TD/13/1032, 1985.

5) See Wu Jiahuang and Cai Tianchang, 'China's Foreign Trade over the past Thirty-five Years', in: *Trade and Development; An UNCTAD Review*, no. 6, 1985 (UN Publications Sales No. E/85/11/D/20).

6) 'Agreement Establishing the Common Fund for Commodities', *UNCTAD Document* TD/IPC/CF/CONF/25, 1981.

7) 'The Substantial New Programme of Action for the 1980s for the Least Developed Countries', in: *Report of the United Nations Conference on the Least Developed Countries*, Paris, 1–14 September 1981 (UN Publication Sales No. E/82/I/8).

8) See Alan v. Deardorff and Robert M. Stern, 'Methods of Measurement of Non-tariff Barriers', *UNCTAD Document* ST/MD/28, 1985.

9) See *Trade and Development Report*, 1984, part II: 'The Evolution of the Trade and Payment Systems', United Nations, New York, 1984 (UN Publication Sales No. E/II/D/23).

10) See 'Services and the Development Process', *UNCTAD Document* TD/B/1008/Rev.1 (UN Publication Sales No. E/85/II/D/13).

11) See Frederick F. Clairmonte and John H. Cavanagh, 'Transnational Corporations and Services: The Final Frontier', in: *Trade and Development; An UNCTAD Review*, No. 5, 1984, pp. 215–273 (UN Publication Sales No. E/F/84/II/D/8).

12) See for an elaboration of this option the report of the independent study-group on problems facing the international trading system (chairman Dr Fritz Leutwiler), *Trade Policies for a Better Future; Proposals for Action*, GATT, Geneva, 1985.

13) M. Wolf, 'Fiddling While the GATT Burns', in: *The World Economy*, Vol. 9, no. 1, March 1986, pp. 1–18.

14) *North–South: A Programme for Survival*, The Report of the Independent Commission on International Development Issues under the Chairmanship of Willy Brandt, Chapter 11, Pan Books, London, 1979.

15) Maurice Bertrand, *Some Reflections on Reform of the United Nations* (JIU/REP/85/9), UN Joint Inspection Unit, Geneva, 1985.

7 The Multilateral Approach to Food Security

Wouter Tims*

There are few areas where contrasts in the world are as sharp as between people's food supplies, with food waste and widespread obesity at one extreme and frequent mass-starvation or permanent undernourishment at the other. Nor are there many areas where the concerns being voiced are so much in contrast with the virtual absence of co-operative international action. The issues concerning the world food situation and the motivation of policies bearing on that issue are touched upon only lightly in this paper. The main question addressed here concerns the role of the international agencies, particularly those under the United Nations' umbrella, in establishing appropriate frameworks for national and international action in the fields of food and agriculture.

Food Security

Although the term 'food security' itself is of recent vintage, it well summarizes the overriding concerns in the field of food. The concept can be defined at different but interrelated levels; not uncommonly in discussions of food issues, a

* *Wouter Tims* is Director of the Centre for World Food Studies at the Free University of Amsterdam. He is an advisor to the Dutch Ministry of Development Co-operation and the Ministry of Agriculture and a member of various international development committees. Between 1973 and 1976 he was Director of the Economic Analysis and Projections Department of the World Bank in Washington, and between 1977 and 1983 a member of the Executive Board of the International Fund for Agricultural Development. He has published extensively on issues in economic development, planning and agricultural and food policies.

particular level is selected implicitly and the concept given content accordingly, omitting other levels and interrelations. This is unfortunate as it leads to analyses and policy concerns which are focused too narrowly. However, the term is now widely used with different connotations which are seldom made explicit. In what follows no attempt is made to replace it with a different term; instead the concept is defined more comprehensively than is usually the case, but without expanding its meaning beyond what the various users of the term may select to bring under it.

First, the concept relates to the food security of people: assuring that everyone has secure access to adequate amounts of nutrition in accordance with physical needs. The human dimension of food security is concerned with stable local supplies of food at affordable prices for all. It includes, therefore, a variety of concerns, especially the following: productive and remunerative employment; distribution of subsidized or free food to those lacking the necessary purchasing power; supplies to vulnerable groups and the intra-household distribution of available food; improvements of the nutritional quality of diets and the need for supplies from outside the local areas; and the transport and storage of supplies, when the region itself is not producing enough food to meet the nutrition requirements of its population. This concept of food security has been the main driving force of food policies, particularly in China.

Second, the concept can also be applied at the national level, where it easily becomes entwined with concerns about the food self-sufficiency of countries. At this level the concept does not relate – or at best only distantly – to the need for food of those deprived of adequate food. Instead, it is addressed to the maintenance of stable and reliable supplies of food for the national market. It translates into efforts to increase national food production and to limit dependence on imported food supplies. With respect to needed imports it is concerned with access to international supplies of food at low and stable prices or in the form of food aid. Food security at the world level is a third dimension which addresses the mutual responsibilities of trading nations to maintain stable market conditions and prices.

Clearly, the three variants of the concept are related to each other. If a government pursues policies to provide food security for its people, the national food balance sheet will be affected as it is necessary for more food to be available than the quantity the market currently absorbs. It may in turn lead to putting a higher priority on accelerating domestic food production and to larger requests for aid, including food aid. In the reverse sense, a government concerned with food security only at the national level may achieve its objectives of stable supplies and prices in domestic food markets without any significant change in the numbers of people inadequately fed.

Definitions of food security can therefore be flawed, if seen in isolation. National or world food security by itself does little or nothing for the permanently hungry; people's food security cannot be achieved, even less maintained, if not complemented by appropriate food policies in the domestic economy. It is therefore logically attractive to define food security in a broad sense, to embrace the individual, national and international levels. This is indeed the concept which will be used here. The reason for covering the elements separately in this introduction is that the term is often used to indicate only one of its aspects. Social scientists concentrate on human needs and often neglect the supplementary measures required nationally to secure food supplies, whereas economists and civil servants tend to look only at national issues and overlook the risk that people's food needs may not be best served by national policies alone. Even international organizations with responsibilities regarding food and agriculture have not escaped from the dangers of using too narrow an interpretation.

The International Food Organizations

The first specialized agency established within the framework of the United Nations was the Food and Agriculture Organization (FAO) in October 1945.[1] The basic declarations preceding and accompanying the establishment of the FAO, all take hunger and poverty as their starting point. The philosophy at the time of its founding was developed in the 1930s and linked the future of agriculture and farm populations to an objective of improved food intake by all people. The misery of farmers during the Depression years, together with the growing awareness of widespread hunger and malnutrition around the globe, were at the root of the creation of FAO. Farmers would be able to produce more if demand for food was raised, both through the markets, by increasing employment and purchasing power, and outside the markets, through internationally co-ordinated procurement of surplus food for distribution at lower prices to those in need.

The supply path of agricultural surplus produced in some parts of the world to the poor and malnourished has many stages and not all of those were seen with equal clarity. The issues which concerned farmers in the surplus countries, notably North America and Australia at that time, were clearest: farmers should be put in a position where a rise in international demand for their outputs would be assured for the purpose of generating reasonable incomes for them. Less clarity existed in respect to international market arrangements, although ideas about buffer stocks, wheat reserves and international stabilisation measures for agricultural markets were being proposed and discussed at the time. In any case, at the end of the Second World War when the FAO was established, it was clear that for some time to come Europe would remain a major importer of food as its agricultural sector could not meet domestic food needs. But no clear views existed regarding ways to reach the even poorer consumers elsewhere in the world, nor who would pay for the subsidies to provide them with food.

A lot has changed, and a lot has been learned since that time. The link between malnutrition (and policies to overcome it) on the one hand, and surplus food production on the other, is no longer thought to exist in the simple, almost naïve, terms which were used in those early years. Much more is understood today about the causes of hunger and malnutrition, particularly in their relation to poverty. Lack of purchasing power to obtain adequate food is at its root, which in turn is related to the lack of opportunities for productive employment, particularly for the unskilled and the uneducated and especially in rural areas. A great deal has been learned about the dynamics of rural development and rural poverty: there is now recognition of the risk that new agricultural technologies for developing countries may, at least for some time after their introduction, not have the desired effect on people's food security because of their potentially distorting effects on the distribution of income and of productive resources.

International measures to redistribute food between surplus and deficit countries through food aid, to stabilise world agricultural markets and to create reserves to be used in times of global scarcity appear, against the background sketched above, in a somewhat different light. Redistribution, stabilisation and emergency reserves were consistently at the centre of attention in international discussions on food, and it should be emphasized now also, that international co-operation on these objectives should not be discarded as irrelevant in solving the world food problem. But, by themselves, they are far from adequate. Over the years there has been growing awareness that such measures can, at best, create more favourable conditions for developing countries, permitting them somewhat more leeway, and less uncertainty, when they pursue policies to alleviate hunger within their own borders. There is much more recognition currently for the twinning of international *and* national policies, to meet the challenge of hunger in the world effectively.

Obviously, the question to be raised here concerns the extent to which the FAO and the other Rome-based UN organizations concerned with world food problems have led the way, both in the gradual uncovering of the roots of that problem and in devising policy options to eradicate it. Unfortunately, one must conclude that such leadership has hardly been the case. Knowledge and understanding within these organizations has followed, rather than spearheaded, the insights gained elsewhere. Even in following the leads from outside, there has been some reluctance or even resistance to giving up views which, as a consequence, are still being defended even when outdated. Policy thinking has been even weaker, inappropriately focused and sometimes demonstrably biased as well. But given the original ideas about the world food problem when the FAO was established, and given the direction which consequently was taken by the organization in selecting its areas of attention, its internal organization and the fields of competence of its staff, this is understandable. The FAO certainly was not unique, as will be noted later, in starting from a set of concepts which gradually were found to be far too simplistic. It was further hampered in adjusting to new insights by the vested interests of staff with competence in an area too narrow to come to grips with the broader dimensions of the world food problem.

We will return to these historical factors and to an analysis of their consequences for the focus of FAO's activities in the next section. At this point it is appropriate to move quickly through the last four decades and to note that in the course of those years several other international organizations were created to perform particular tasks concerning food and agriculture. The first of these was the World Food Programme (WFP), also based in Rome, created in 1961. It is a rather logical outgrowth of the basic premises of the FAO: to dispose of surplus food of developed countries, particularly when the worst of European food problems were a thing of the past. Balance-of-payments constraints and limited credit-worthiness of food-deficit countries required that food should be made available as aid, on the 'softest' possible terms. The new multilateral agency resulted from a reshuffling of functions, as the WFP was set up under the joint responsibility of the UN Secretary General and the FAO's Director General. It was expected to lead the way in assessing needs, in exploring appropriate mechanisms and channels for food aid and, in the process, guiding bilateral food aid donors.

A burst of new initiatives occurred in 1974 at the World Food Conference which coincided with one of the worst food crises in South Asia. At that time export supplies of food from elsewhere were low and international prices climbed to high levels. Apart from resolutions urging more food aid and the establishment of international stabilisation measures in the grain markets, three new organizations were proposed and subsequently established. The first was the World Food Council which was given the task of regular high-level consultation on national and international policies affecting the world food situation. A limited number of countries, some permanently represented and others rotating within country groupings, constituted the body which was expected to be of considerable stature.

Through its deliberations and recommendations it was expected to exert significant influence over a broad array of international organizations charged with responsibilities for international co-operation in the fields of food and agriculture. An important feature was membership of the USSR and other East European countries which were absent from FAO but had influenced the world food situation profoundly by their greatly increased food imports which began in the early 1970s.

The second one was the International Fund for Agricultural Development (IFAD), a lending agency endowed for the first three years of its operation with an amount of about $1 billion. Proposals to create a fund of this kind had been tabled earlier, but Western donor countries were reluctant to agree as they maintained objections to any financial organization under the United Nations with its 'one country, one vote' system. Earlier, in 1960, they had shown that preference most clearly when creating the International Development Association (IDA) under the auspices of the World Bank, where contributions determine votes, rather than agreeing to the creation of a similar fund within the United Nations. An important reason for donor countries to be more forthcoming with regard to IFAD's creation was the opportunity it created to attract part of the substantial balance-of-payments surpluses of the oil-exporting countries into multilateral aid channels. The industrialized countries proposed parity of contributions between themselves and the oil-exporting countries and equal voting rights for both country groups. Both groups subsequently agreed each to transfer one-third of their votes to the remaining developing countries, thus creating three country groups with equal voting rights. Interestingly, the donors can muster two-thirds of the total votes, but equally the developing countries (including the oil-exporters again) have a two-thirds share.

The third new organization was the Consultative Group for Food Production and Investment (CGFPI). It was modelled on another Consultative Group, the International Agricultural Research (CGIAR) body which had been established in 1968 by the FAO and the World Bank. The latter's purpose, very successfully pursued, was to bring donors together for the support of a growing number of international research institutes involved in the development of new technologies for agricultural food crops (especially seeds) in the developing countries. The CGIAR had private organizations as donors, together with interested governments, but the CGFPI – in which the UNDP, the FAO and the World Bank shared the secretarial responsibilities – was set up purely with government responsibilities. The basic idea was to mobilise resources for agricultural development in general, in the same way as was done earlier for agricultural research.

This organization met with considerable problems almost from the beginning, as donors already provided aid for agriculture in the context of their own relations with individual recipient countries, and co-ordinated with other donors through the mechanism of country-specific consultative groups. The risk of duplication or conflicting decisions made donors reluctant to take the new forum entirely seriously. In order to focus the discussions, a select number of developing countries was urged to submit national food strategies as a basis for eliciting donor support, but again this seemed more appropriately discussed in country-specific consultative groups and ultimately led to a consensus to abolish the CGFPI in 1978. The idea of national food strategies was later taken over and strongly promoted by the World Food Council.

Finally, one should note that multilateral activities in food and agriculture also play a major role in the World Bank and in the three regional development banks for Latin America, Asia and Africa. In the early 1960s the World Bank began to provide finance for agricultural development; during the most recent decade this constituted about 30 per cent of the World Bank's lending activities and a similar proportion of the activities of the regional banks. Logically, the FAO claimed that it could provide all the technical support required for the preparation of agricultural projects which the World Bank considered eligible for financing. The World Bank doubted the quality of the FAO's support and proposed instead a co-operative programme with staff located at the FAO but selected and largely financed by the World Bank. Later, when more financing agencies began to use the same kind of arrangement with the FAO, this co-operative programme became the FAO's Investment Centre. About one third of the World Bank's new projects in the field of agriculture and rural development are normally prepared by this wing of the FAO: if 'repeater' projects (those which require no direct support for their preparation) are included, that share is raised to two thirds. The FAO also acts as an executive agency for technical assistance projects in its field which are financed by the UNDP.

Thus, over the past four decades a network of international organizations has gradually been established with particular responsibilities for improving the world food situation and promoting agricultural development. Their competence covers a broad area and their capabilities range from international policy analysis to the specifics of preparing and financing development projects and providing food aid. The relevance of this organizational competence must ultimately be judged by asking: to what extent can it contribute to the eradication of hunger and the provision of food security to all human beings? That issue will now be considered by tracing the evolution of thinking on the subject and the direction of action over the course of the years. Judgements about the multilateral organizations and their usefulness must then be drawn from such an analysis.

The Multilateral Organizations and Food Security

The main thesis presented here is that the multilateral agencies, during the past four decades, have been largely concerned with the food security of nations rather than of people. This has resulted in a focus being placed on food-importing countries on the production side of the food balance and on international initiatives to provide food aid and to stabilise world agricultural markets.

Attention to issues of food consumption policy and internal distribution of food has been marginal by comparison. This thesis will be supported by an analysis of the main currents discernible in some of the major documents issued by the various multilateral organizations, the actions of such organizations which are considered to be of primary importance, and the main concerns of the organizations as these find expression in their separate programmes. Most of the discussion will concentrate on trends over roughly the last 15 years; this is the period during which the poverty issue was rediscovered as the core problem of development, but then receded again under the pressure of a deteriorating international environment which made national economic problems again more prominent.

One should be careful with the interpretation of the proposed thesis: it would be all too easy to conclude that multilateral organizations concerned with food have not lived up to their basic responsibility in that they have limited their view of food security largely to the national level. Before coming to such a conclusion, one needs to ask the question: to what extent are these organizations really in a position to choose their own interpretations and objectives? The fact that national member governments are the organizations' constituency, and that the nations present their own views of the issues and exercise their influence in decision making about the priorities to be set for these organizations, considerably limits the options of multilateral organizations.

Particularly in the area of food and agriculture there are sensitivities within this relationship with national governments which are hard to deal with. Governments of developing countries face a set of constraining factors on their own activities which they tend to bring forward as their first and foremost concern in any international forum. They are often concerned about their ability to maintain and enlarge agricultural exports and to obtain remunerative prices for those products, partly because an important part of their fiscal resources depends on those exports. They want to be sure of access to international supplies of food at affordable prices and financed with aid flows if their purchasing power and credit-worthiness is limited. These aid flows are also desired because of the local currency counterpart funds which they can generate, strengthening their fiscal position. And, last but not least, there is a strong political incentive to ensure adequate supplies of food at stable prices to urban consumers, regardless of the origin of those supplies. It is this set of problems faced by member governments which tends to determine the agenda of the multilateral organizations concerned with food.

When the focus is changed and put on security for all people and particularly for the poorest amongst them, then the agenda changes considerably. Questions are then raised as to why large groups of people are poor and hungry, which in turn leads to questions about the distribution of productive endowments: land, access to education, to agricultural credit, extension and research. Issues such as land reform, the distribution of benefits from irrigation and from new seed-based technologies, together with the review of agricultural support services, then become crucial. Such a focus also more effectively reveals the set of food distribution policies and the spread of benefits from food subsidies. All of these issues are clearly of a domestic kind and most governments prefer to deal with them independently rather than to have them discussed in international fora.

Multilateral organizations thus face pressures from their developing country members against raising issues which they consider to be largely or entirely of a domestic nature, and with which their governments should be left to deal without interference. They also face pressure to raise issues which require action by the developed countries and which promise to ease the constraints on foreign exchange and fiscal resources which limit the capacity of developing country governments to pursue their own objectives. In this situation it is clearly not feasible for any multilateral organization to go far beyond the national-level interpretation of the food security concept without invoking the wrath of a majority of its membership. Judgements about the way multilateral organizations have conducted their business should put considerable weight on this aspect of their position.

Although structures of this kind apply for all international organizations, some have had a better opportunity to determine their own areas of priority concern. The degree of dependence on national budget support has played an important role in that respect. This issue of emphasis on international, rather than national measures, promises benefits to governments of developing countries to the detriment of focus on domestic policies which promise to benefit the most deprived people. The entire discussion elsewhere in the UN system about a New International Economic Order, the rights and responsibilities of States and the particular proposals discussed in this connection are in the same vein and by themselves hold little promise for the poor. What has been constantly missing is a clear and commonly-accepted understanding that the only reasonable way to improve international economic co-operation is to put the national policies of all countries on the agenda; a common willingness to change these policies would open perspectives for the use of additional resources for development to the benefit of the most needy people. Opinions about the most desirable or efficient ways to do so may differ, but international support for development will remain only lukewarm if developing countries do not show more willingness to discuss and, where deemed necessary, to adjust their own policies. In the UN system this complementarity has never received sufficient emphasis, not least because the majority of its membership remains unwilling to recognize reciprocity as a dominant feature of international relations and instead perseveres in demanding privileged treatment. One must add, at the same time, that countries other than developing countries have reacted in a similar manner when international organizations have put their domestic policies on the agenda, such as their trade and aid policies, for example, which arise in the context of UNCTAD.

The focus on the macroeconomic aspects of food problems, and on international measures to ease them, fits neatly into this preferred view of the world economy. Such a focus provides an argument for skirting international debates on appropriate national policies to alleviate hunger and malnutrition. International measures and proposals have remained at the core of the debate with respect to food in the multilateral organizations, particularly those based in Rome. The orientation of the organizations, towards the supply-side of the food balance has expressed itself also in the particular expertise which has been established both among their staff and in their programmes of action.

In the multilateral banks, particularly the World Bank, the situation has been somewhat different as its lending for agricultural development, with its stringent preconditions of sound economic returns and technical feasibility of projects, did require negotiations to instigate changes of policies and to promote institutional reforms. Conditions negotiated concerning projects did not remain restricted to the specific needs directly related to project implementation but concerned also issues of sector or even macroeconomic policies like pricing, border policies and taxation or the allocation of investment resources. Until the mid-1970s these conditions were, in the main, related to improving the mobilisation and efficient use of resources; subsequently the issue of the distribution of benefits from these projects also became a more important criterion.

In order to be able to negotiate on these issues, multilateral banks need to acquire and maintain a thorough understanding of the structure of each borrowing country's economy. In this respect a major difference can be observed compared with the Rome-based organizations, the latter having much less country-specific knowledge, particularly regarding the sets of policies which governments pursue and their effects on food production and distribution.

Although the particular concerns of the World Bank did entail an involvement with national food policies, this did not necessarily lead to a focus on people's food security. Even when the World Bank, particularly after 1973, began to address issues of poverty and hunger more directly, it did not shift all of its lending towards the alleviation of the poverty problem, for several reasons. It would have been practically impossible to do so as data and knowledge were scarce and, therefore, national poverty-oriented lending was more difficult. A reorientation of its own staff was needed and that also took considerable time. Not least, borrowing countries were reluctant to make more than marginal changes in their own priorities. The World Bank had, therefore, to find acceptable compromises: some projects are called 'rural development projects' when there is reasonable assurance that a major section of the total beneficiaries is poor, whereas others are labelled 'agricultural projects' when the distribution of project benefits appears less directed to the poor but technical and economic feasibility criteria are still met. Both types of projects can exist side by side and it depends on the understandings reached with borrowing governments how a balance is struck between the two.

The UN organizations concerned with food and agriculture have also from time to time put issues connected with the internal policies in developing countries on the agenda. Conferences were organized on land reform and on rural development on at least two occasions and agreement was found on a number of useful recommendations. In somewhat broader terms, the UN resolutions with regard to the Second and Third Development Decades have not eschewed statements regarding domestic policy adjustments in all countries. However, there has never been a strong and well-staffed multilateral follow-up, to see how the agreed policies were put into practice. There was never the need, as in the case of the World Bank, to build up detailed country knowledge or to monitor policies affecting the agricultural sector or the food situation and the conferences did not lead to any significant changes in that respect.

As a consequence, the international fora dealing with the issue of food security have only met the challenges halfway and have not fully recognized the need to discuss simultaneously the domestic policy adjustments in member countries needed to meet the food needs of the poor, and the international policies which are conducive and supportive to this kind of development policy. This is unfortunate as it has adversely affected international decisions which as a consequence have tended to be too exclusively addressed to the richer countries in asking for restraints on the latter's policies and for the mobilisation of larger resources for the benefit of the developing countries. These were not matched by much of a commitment on the part of the developing countries to pursue policies promising a better deal for their poor, more resources for agricultural and rural development or even a reasonably efficient use of these resources generally. The willingness of the richer countries to comply with these requests was, and remains, strictly limited. In fact, the whole approach provided them with an argument to justify their meagre responses.

It is also unfortunate because a disjointed discussion of international measures also leads to wrong priorities and proposals. Thus, it leads, for example, to attaching priority to the group of food deficit, low-income countries when providing external assistance, both for food aid and assistance to accelerate agricultural production growth. Having a food deficit, of course, does not necessarily imply that a country is pursuing domestic policies to alleviate hunger, in which case increasing the supply of food in those countries may not help to improve the food security for the poor. Conversely, the fact that a country is not a net importer of food does not in any way imply that there are no people who face severe insecurities with respect to their food supplies; Thailand and Pakistan are prime examples of this phenomenon, with India having joined this group more recently and other Asian countries moving in the same direction. Some of these countries do make considerable efforts to alleviate poverty and hunger and are, therefore, worthy recipients of larger flows of aid, but the fact that they do not import food would omit them from the list of countries which are to be given priority!

In fact, this whole concept of food deficit countries leads the discussion and the focus of action astray, as it loses sight of the problems of developing countries which, in growing numbers, are becoming food self-sufficient but still harbour large numbers of poor and hungry people. Obviously, food aid is not a suitable instrument and additional aid to accelerate their food production is not very useful either. Both may lead to a fall of food prices in the domestic market, large enough to operate as a disincentive to farmers and to reduce the growth of production. What is needed in that situation (particularly when exporting food surpluses is an unlikely solution because of infrastructural handicaps and inadequate quality for external sales) is subsidized domestic distribution targeted to the poor, and accelerated economic growth to promote domestic demand for all agricultural products. Both of these measures require additional resources, at least initially, to a large extent from abroad. These resources should not be provided as food aid, but rather in the form of programme aid support, which permits the government to meet the demand for non-food imports which is unavoidably generated by these policies. The focus on food deficit countries completely loses sight of these issues.

The detrimental effects of starting the discussion from the viewpoint of international issues can also be seen clearly in the shift it has caused in aid flows away from Asia and towards Africa, which presently is the largest low-income, food-deficit region. This criticism is not intended to in any way belittle the problems which are facing sub-Saharan Africa, but it draws attention to the inappropriateness − to say the least − of assuming that the gradual disappearance of food imports in South and Southeast Asia is a reason to assume that aid can be shifted elsewhere. Aid flows to these two regions are presently about equal, notwithstanding the fact that the number of people with energy-deficient diets in Asia is almost three times as large as in sub-Saharan Africa. It is well accepted that aid to Asia cannot contain much food aid and should be focused less strongly on agricultural development than in Africa, but the magnitude of the remaining poverty problem in Asia, the opportunities to support poverty-alleviating programmes in that part of the world and the need to accelerate its growth as a condition for continued agricultural progress all indicate the need for much larger aid flows to South Asia. Certainly this should not be at the expense of Africa by reversing past trends, but should be achieved more by a general increase of aid in suitable forms which is based on a better understanding of needs and opportunities than the concept of food deficit countries permits.

Recent Signs of Change

In recent years the debates have shown a shift in the relative importance of issues concerning international measures in the field of food and agriculture. In some respects such shifts may be interpreted as healthy signs, as a more balanced view may be emerging about priorities, responsibilities and new ways for productive co-operation towards alleviating the food problem.

When, in the late 1960s, new agricultural technologies began to be adopted in South and Southeast Asia and the production of wheat, then rice and, more recently, a number of other food products, began to increase rapidly, the results were not uniformly judged to be positive. Although the fear that greater inequalities would result from faster adoption of new technologies by larger rather than by smaller farmers appeared with hindsight to be unjustified, there still remain lingering doubts about the consequences of these new technologies on the poor. As summarized by Lipton and Longhurst in their recent survey of evidence for the CGIAR, [2] the new technologies did lose a good deal of their 'pro-poor' characteristics by their insertion into social systems favouring urban groups and big farmers, whereas at the same time demographic dynamics (including migration) make labour cheaper relative to land. As food producers, the poor gained less than larger producers in areas where new technologies were introduced; also most poor farmers in South Asia and Africa live outside those areas. As consumers, they tended to gain through lower prices − if increased production was not offset by lower imports − whereas in the case of landless labourers in rural areas, their wages have hardly improved as larger demand for labour was largely met through migration to areas adopting new technologies.

The uneasiness about the effects of the 'green revolution' on the poor did, with the benefit of hindsight, have some grounding. A balanced and comprehensive review, such as the quoted document, demonstrates that economic growth, including the growth of agricultural production, does not necessarily benefit the poor, and is unlikely to increase their income at rates comparable to those of higher income groups. 'Trickle down' occurs, but not at a rate sufficient to give present generations of the poor hope of escaping their predicament. What kind of measures and approaches could accelerate the participation of the poor in the development process? McNamara raised that question forcefully in his presidential address to the annual meeting of the World Bank's members in Nairobi in 1973 and outlined a programme designed to benefit the rural poor more directly through projects specifically geared to their needs. But it was expected to take many years to achieve that objective, as the staff of the World Bank, traditionally concerned more with technical feasibility and returns in terms of added production, was uneasy with equity issues and with the policy assessments associated with them. The practical difficulties encountered – including developing country governments' trepidation – led to slow progress, whereas in recent years other concerns like energy and adjustment to a changing world economy have taken precedence in the activities of the World Bank.

The next year, 1974, witnessed the World Food Conference, one of the most productive of a long list of such meetings throughout the 1970s. A main feature remained, however, the overriding concern with international issues and the lack of attention to the food needs of the poor. These were continuously cited, but then the discourses referred only in passing to national policies to alleviate poverty and, as usual, jumped straight into discussions of food aid, agricultural assistance and trade measures, and the need for high-level policy co-ordination. In all these areas much was achieved in an organizational sense: creation of the World Food Council for policy discussions at the ministerial level; the Committee on Food Aid Policies and Programmes (CFA) and the Committee on Food Security (CFS), both attached to FAO; the Consultative Group on Food Production and Investment (CGFPI) and the foundation was laid for the International Fund for Agricultural Development (IFAD) which in 1977 reached its minimum funding and started its operations in 1978. After 1973/74 the change concerning perceptions of the world food problem as enunciated from Rome progressed exceedingly slowly. In 1980, at the Arusha meeting of the World Food Council, the basic documents referred for the first time to consumption policies as a complement to the objective of raising production. In the next year though, the FAO's long-term outlook document 'Agriculture, Towards 2000' was strongly supply-oriented, expecting about two-thirds of increased food production to be obtained from irrigated land and blithely assuming that this would raise all rural incomes at the same rate, thus reducing poverty and hunger. In the meantime, the International Fund for Agricultural Development established innovative approaches to the elevation of the rural poor as the centre point of its lending activities and demonstrated, though on a modest scale, that it is possible to mobilise small farmers to support initiatives taken by themselves to improve their food security. In 1983 the Committee on Food Security of the FAO [3] finally did change its concept of food security, stating: 'The ultimate objective of world food security should be to ensure that all people have both physical and economic access to the basic food they need'. It then translated this principle into three specific aims: '... ensuring production of adequate food supplies; maximizing stability in the flow of supplies; and securing access to available supplies on the part of those who need them'. However appealing this new concept is, the implementation of the third aim remains open-ended.

Out of the 73 (!) paragraphs which, in the same document, are devoted to 'possible measures', two concern access of consumers. One paragraph says that rural employment should be promoted, the other refers to food-for-work programmes to subsidize distribution measures. There is no recognition of the link between such domestic policies and the necessary external support to make those programmes possible.

In essence, is is hardly an overstatement to say that new approaches to food security in their full sense originate largely outside the FAO: in terms of practical ways to reach the poor, the IFAD has led the way, whereas in terms of overall policies by developed and developing countries, the WFC has been significantly more progressive. But both are small and vulnerable: the first because its funding formula is based on a large contribution from the oil-exporting countries which face difficulties in maintaining their share; the second because the FAO considers that the WFC operates too independently, and not, as originally intended 'within the framework of the FAO'. There is bitterness in the FAO, both for having been denied any control over the resources now channelled to the IFAD and for having to live with an organization discussing policies at the ministerial level outside its direct authority.

The World Bank, which for a long time has remained rather silent on the issue, recently published its own views on food security[4] putting the needs of people squarely at the centre and recognizing the developmental importance of consumption policies which improve food access for the poor. However, taking a broad view of the discussions, one cannot but sympathize with a statement made at the June 1984 meeting of the WFC in Addis Ababa by the International Council of Voluntary Agencies: 'The international community is still far too obsessed with food issues such as agricultural trade, food security in terms of global stock and investment in food production. These do not necessarily focus on hunger and malnutrition, and the rural poor have little, if any, voice in shaping either international or national agenda on food'. And on the WFC its adds: 'being a political forum, it has the undoubted capacity to shape a more relevant agenda'. The final paragraphs of this paper will attempt to answer the question as to whether this can be achieved in the years to come.

Prospects for Hunger-Alleviating Policies

What is needed is a thorough rethinking of the implications, in policy terms, of a broad interpretation of food security which starts from people's needs and builds up from there to the local, national and international priorities to achieve their fulfillment. That kind of comprehensive analysis is rare and far from easy to accomplish, due to time and staff requirements, lack of appropriate sets of data, and differing policy priorities of governments. Thus, the incentive to undertake this work is lacking. The World Bank has, in the course of time, undertaken studies of this kind but these were usually not sufficiently collaborative with policy-making bodies in the countries concerned to make them into a permanent tool for national policy analysis. Similar studies done in the 1960s and early 1970s by the ILO also had only a temporary impact. The FAO has not moved beyond modelling of production, demand and international trade. For example, the country models constructed for its study 'Agriculture, Towards 2000' do not differentiate between income groups and their food supplies and, therefore, are not suitable to analyse issues of food security for the poor.

Improved analyses are needed to get to grips with the implications of broadly defined food security. The techniques are available and have been tested by now in a few cases. A comprehensive study done by the Bangladesh Planning Commission with support from the Centre for World Food Studies in Amsterdam demonstrates not only the feasibility of comprehensiveness but also provides some new and rather unexpected insights. It suggests that a rapid expansion of subsidized food distribution to the poor, assuming an acceptable and realistic degree of leakage to non-target groups, can put a burden on the government budget which reduces the capacity of public investment significantly and retards economic growth. If, however, additional aid is provided which permits meeting the cost of food subsidies and at the same time maintains the level of public investment, long-term growth would be accelerated. The additional aid meets the demand spilling over into imports and it is interesting to note that the additional import demand is less than one quarter for food, the other three-quarters of demand being for non-food goods and services. Apparently, the simple idea that aid intended to support a government programme of subsidized food distribution can largely be provided as food aid is incorrect; in fact, food aid can only meet a minor part of the additional aid required whereas the rest must be in the form of programme aid or balance-of-payments support.

These findings are supported by a similar study done by Parikh and Narayana for India (forthcoming) which leads to virtually the same conclusion about the required composition of additional aid. If donors and recipients act on the mistaken assumption that food aid can be the main instrument, they risk oversupplying the food market and causing a deterioration in the internal agricultural terms of trade which may act in turn as a disincentive to production of food for the market.

The need for similar analyses in other countries should be obvious, irrespective of whether they import food or not, as long as there are significant groups of people in those countries suffering from inadequate food intake. Analyses of this kind are also needed in order to make sure that aid policies are properly dovetailed to the changes in demand patterns which occur when subsidized food distribution to the poor (through whatever type of programme or approach) is initiated or expanded by the government. Food aid may play a role, but on a more modest scale than usually thought.

These findings strike at the heart of the concerns and objectives pursued by the FAO and, to some extent, the World Food Council. Their emphasis on food deficit countries is inappropriate, but they also express too much faith in food aid as an instrument to improve food security. More tenable positions in these respects require that these organizations take a much larger interest in the domestic policies – in a rather broad sense – of low-income countries, collect more information on the area and devote more resources to strengthening the capacity within these countries to carry out domestic policy analysis. As far as the FAO is concerned, it means that a bridge must be built between, at one end, the work on the food security of nations in a global context and, at the other end, the work done on the preparation of agricultural projects. The gap to be bridged concerns the domestic policies which bear on both agriculture and on the food security of the poor.

Recently, at the UN Special Sessions on Africa, there was a heartening willingness on the part of African governments to put their own policies on the international agenda. They demonstrated in that way a changed perception of their situation and of the causes of their predicaments which do not have exclusively external origins, thereby requiring a solution imposed from outside. They are beginning to open the door to more reciprocity, to show willingness to accept advice on their own policies in exchange for more support from outside to ease the transitional frictions. It is much too early to say whether this will become a new trend, as openness is an easier thing to express than to practise and as donors do not have a very good track record in providing the needed additional aid for adjustment.

Still, it provides an opportunity, for the FAO in particular, to provide assistance to countries which are willing to adopt policies to improve people's food security. National food strategies which link production and consumption concerns, need to be developed and appropriate aid packages must be identified to support their implementation. In its recent study 'Poverty and Hunger' (1986) the World Bank recognizes consumption policies as a legitimate part of development policies and a joint approach of the two multilateral agencies should therefore be possible and attractive. The World Bank has a long tradition in country policy analysis, whereas in the FAO this needs to be established. The need for strengthening the core economic management agencies in low-income countries has already been stressed by aid donors for many years; these countries, as FAO members, should add their weight to directing the FAO towards. establishing its own assistance capability. When centred around the concept of people's food security, the FAO could help developing countries to approach their food problems more effectively, use external resources more directly geared to solving that problem and to focus more clearly on priorities for international co-operation.

The FAO is the largest specialized agency of the UN system. It carries a great responsibility for the way the system as a whole is seen and judged. A concept of food security which tends to emphasize what the rich countries ought to do to ease the macroeconomic problems of developing country governments is bound to lead to indecisiveness and reluctance in changing trade and aid policies, especially when the developing countries are not seen to be making complementary policy changes. Focusing upon people's food needs leads to conclusions about joint action opportunities by all countries together, ultimately promising the eradication of hunger by the turn of this century. The FAO should be at the centre of the process by expanding its span of policy analysis and its assistance capabilities in that field, and thus strengthening the argument of the developing countries for greatly enhanced international support measures.

To do this effectively, FAO needs to change its attitudes towards co-operation with the World Bank and with other UN agencies. The problems to be faced and the tasks to be performed are of a magnitude exceeding the capacity of any of them separately, maybe even their joint strengths. Food problems are embedded in a complex network and must be understood and tackled in their wider context. An attitude which is more like the defence of a fiefdom than the readiness to co-operate and to learn from others is not helpful and jeopardizes progress towards eradicating hunger.

Notes

1) As became the standard to be applied to other specialized agencies when those were established in later years, a Relationship Agreement was signed with the United Nations (in 1945), which stipulates that the Economic and Social Council (ECOSOC) of the United Nations is the co-ordinating body.
2) Michael Lipton and Richard Longhurst, 'Modern Varieties, International Agricultural Research, and the Poor', *CGIAR Study Paper* No. 2, The World Bank, Washington DC, October 1985.
3) Committee on World Food Security, Eighth Session, April 1983: 'Director-General's Report on World Security: A reappraisal of the Concepts and Approaches', *CFS*, FAO, Rome, 1983/4.
4) *Poverty and Hunger: Issues and Options for Food Security in Developing Countries*, World Bank, Washington, 1986.

8 The International Labour Organization as a Development Agency

Louis Emmerij*

Introduction

The only claim I have to discuss the International Labour Organization (ILO) is that I worked there for almost six years; the only claim I have to discuss the intriguing notion of the ILO as a *development agency* is that during my years at the ILO I directed the organization's World Employment Programme (WEP). Let me say from the outset that I had to put up a fight in order to keep the 'traditional' ILO at a distance in order that the 'new' ILO would be able to survive. In the end I believe I lost the battle. It is this tension between the old and the new or between two ideologies – which I will later refer to as the ideology of the structure of the organization and the ideology of the programme – which will run as a leitmotiv throughout this chapter.

This chapter will be divided into five parts:

1.   The origin of the ILO.

* *Louis Emmerij* is currently President of the Development Centre of the Organization for Economic Co-operation and Development. From 1971 to 1976 he was Director of the World Employment Programme at the International Labour Organization. Between 1976 and 1986 he was Rector of the Institute of Social Studies, The Hague. He has written extensively on economic development, education, and social policy and also directed research in these fields.

2. The two main instruments of action which the ILO has at its disposal: the conventions and the standard setting on the one hand and the technical activities on the other.
3. The World Employment Programme – the ILO as a real development agency.
4. The tension between the two ideologies mentioned above.
5. Finally, the topic will be broadened to include some relevant material for the overall title of the book – *The UN Under Attack*.

Origin and Purpose of the ILO

The ILO is one of the older international organizations. In 1919 the Treaty of Versailles led to the creation of the Permanent Court of International Justice as well as the International Labour Organization with *39 member countries*. Peace and Social Justice was the theme after the First World War, and it was also the principal concern of these two entities. The stated objective was, therefore, to promote peace among nations through the achievement of social justice and amelioration of conditions of labour: international peace through international means. The United States had played, through its trade unions under the active leadership of Samuel Gompers of the American Federation of Labour (AFL), a very active role in setting up the organization but did not join the ILO until 1934. The American Employers, in contrast, claimed: 'The ILO is an instrument of international socialism'. The USSR also initially did not join claiming that: 'The ILO is a capitalistic device to oppress the working people'. This was 1919–1920: there appears to be nothing new under the sun.

The modern history of the ILO probably started in 1944 with the Declaration of Philadelphia. This is a famous declaration which contains the immortal words: 'Poverty anywhere is a threat to prosperity everywhere'. The Declaration of Philadelphia has been appended to the ILO Constitution as a basic statement of purpose. In 1946 the ILO became a specialized agency of the United Nations, after having made a bid for power, though this Declaration of Philadelphia, to take over the entire social and economic activities of what later became the United Nations. In the ILO Constitution and the Statement of Purpose is found a strange mixture of specificity and marvellous vistas. For example, the preamble to the Constitution contains the following examples of specific purposes:

- regulation of working hours, including a maximum working-day and working-week;
- prevention of unemployment;
- securing an adequate living wage;
- preventing occupational disease and injury;
- protection of children, young persons and women;

- protection of interests of those working in countries other than their own;
- equal pay for equal work;
- freedom of association;
- organizational, vocational and technical education.

The Declaration of Philadelphia, as already indicated, amplified these specific purposes and directions. The Declaration quite clearly went into a broader development orientation. For example, full employment and improved living standards and provision for migration and training, so that workers can be employed at their full skills, tend to strike one as being even rather modern concerns. Extension of social security to provide basic income and medical care, provision for adequate nutrition, housing, equality of educational and vocational opportunities – the basic functions of the whole UN social and economic system – is implied in this bid for power contained in the Declaration of Philadelphia appended to the ILO Constitution.

Out of the freedom of association objective – essentially the right of workers to form unions – later emerged the fundamental human rights movement. Out of the Declaration of Philadelphia statements on nutrition, housing, education, came what later became known as basic needs. In short, the political objective of human rights, the economic and social objectives of employment and basic needs, all of that was already implied in the 1919 Constitution and then reinforced in the appended Declaration of Philadelphia of 1944.

In relation to the structure of the ILO: the ILO is the only organization that is not just a governmental organization: apart from government representatives, employers' associations and trade unions also sit around the table. The International Labour Conference meets once a year and brings together two government representatives, one employer and one trade unionist per country. It is also interesting to note that the ILO Governing Body (also with the 2 + 1 + 1 structure), meets three times a year and has a kind of variation of the weighted voting system, by retaining as permanent members 10 countries of 'chief industrial importance'. These countries are: Canada, the People's Republic of China, France, the Federal Republic of Germany, India, Italy, Japan, the USSR, the United Kingdom and the United States. Within the ILO there continues to be a struggle between the annual Conference, which affords no special privileges to any member State, and the Governing Body over the continued acceptance of the permanent members. The Conference wishes to end the practice but the ferocious resistance of the 10 countries concerned has so far been successful in keeping the structure intact.

Instruments of Action

The two instruments of action of the ILO are Conventions and Recommendations and technical assistance activities. The heart of the ILO has always been considered to be the standard-setting activities. The elaboration of Conventions and Recommendations has now resulted in an International Labour Code of approximately 160 Conventions. Technical assistance became a major activity only since 1960.

Conventions and recommendations

Conventions and Recommendations – the standard-setting activities – is very original and interesting work even if I do not agree with much of it. The difference between Recommendations and Conventions is that Recommendations are exploratory instruments while Conventions, once they are adopted, are supposed to be ratified by Parliaments, or more broadly by the competent authorities within the member countries, within 12 to 18 months after the adoption by the International Labour Conference in Geneva.

There exists a very interesting and original piece of compliance machinery. The ILO has set up a well organized series of arrangements by which it can 'police' the progress of implementation within nation states of the International Conventions that are adopted by the International Labour Conferences. These are as follows:

1. There is a double discussion in two successive years; if everything goes well in the second year, a Convention is adopted.
2. The next step is that the Convention must be ratified by the competent authorities in the member countries.
3. Approximately every two years countries must report on the progress made in terms of implementation, even those countries which have not ratified.
4. The reports of individual countries go to an ILO Committee of Experts. That Committee can make 'observations' to the Conference and to the country in question. For example, at one point the USSR was asked to explain legislation concerning 'Persons leading a parasitic way of life'. The answer can be imagined but it is important that this kind of question can be asked.
5. Any trade union or employers' association of any member country may make a 'Representation' to the Governing Body of the ILO – which simply means that they can complain. They can go to the Governing Body and say, for instance, that their government is not enforcing or is confused about this or that Convention. Such complaints are taken very seriously and are examined by a tripartite committee of the Governing Body, which reports to the International Labour Conference.
6. A special list of countries that have failed to comply is published and is therefore public. One can react by arguing that, the USSR, or the USA, or even The Netherlands would not be very much impressed by 'Representations', by 'Observations', blacklists, being published, etc. That

may be true. Nevertheless, there is a certain amount of pressure applied. Many countries do not like being put on a published list in which their non-compliance with accepted and agreed upon Conventions and Recommendations is exposed. Compliance is not compulsory, but this list is an ingenious and effective instrument for putting pressure on governments to comply with the internationally agreed upon Conventions and Recommendations.

Obviously, conventions were originally really meant for, and this can also be seen in their different titles, and indeed focused on, the organized labour groups in the industrialized countries, which are relatively homogeneous groups in relatively homogeneous countries.

After World War II with the huge increase in and growing heterogeneity of member countries, the standard-setting activities of the ILO ran into trouble, precisely because of this growing heterogeneity and the subsequent increasing difficulties of maintaining Conventions as homogeneous instruments used to set standards for countries that were often at very different stages of development. I mentioned already that there are now about 160 Conventions. Some countries ratify them just for purposes of external relations – they have no real desire to implement them. Other countries do not sign for legal reasons. For example, the country that made the most difficulties in my time at the ILO was the United States. It even left the ILO. In total, it only ratified seven of the 160 Conventions. The representatives claim that this is due to legal considerations because at the federal level one cannot ratify Conventions that, according to US law, should be ratified at State level.

This growing heterogeneity of countries and this growing number of Conventions has led to the search for a minimum package of labour standards. Could one visualize that out of these 160 Conventions, which cannot possibly be applicable to all countries in all circumstances, it would be possible to identify a minimum package that would be universally valid?[1] What are the reasons in favour and what are the reasons against the search for, and the adoption of, such a minimum package?

In favour there are three reasons. First, a certain amount of social progress should go hand in hand with economic progress. Second is the solidarity reason: industrialized countries within the ILO should put pressure on developing countries to improve their labour conditions. Putting aside for the moment the unfair competition argument and looking at it from a positive point of view, for reasons of solidarity industrialized countries should put pressure on the governments of developing countries in order to improve the labour conditions there within the international context of the ILO. Third, such a move might go against protectionist tendencies, because the argument of unfair competition can no longer be maintained. But of course, it might be said that this is a hidden form of protectionism.

Here we come to the *reasons against*. First, there are those who maintain that the real reasons for putting pressure on developing countries to improve their labour conditions is in defence of the rich countries' economies. For example, the US trade union federation, the American Federation of Labour and Congress of Industrial Organizations (AFL-CIO), has always attacked the unfair competition of developing countries in the US market, claiming that their own members were pushed out of work, because these other countries did not comply with the international labour standards. But this is really a protectionist argument on the part of the US trade unions.

Second, a premature introduction of minimum standards would lead to the loss of comparative advantages of developing countries.

Finally, the last argument against a minimum standards package is that it would stimulate the creation of a labour aristocracy, would increase labour costs, would increase capital intensity resulting in less overall employment and higher labour market dualism.

Here we are at the very heart of the development problem: employed versus unemployed; modern versus traditional; organized versus unorganized; formal sector versus informal sector. It is noteworthy that the identification of these fundamental dilemmas came out of a discussion which took as a starting point the traditional ILO work on Conventions and Recommendations.

Technical assistance

The second main instrument of the ILO is that of technical assistance. The ILO was one of the first organizations to move into technical assistance, because it was seen as an integral part of the introduction of Conventions in countries. Thus, already at an early stage, technical assistance was seen by the ILO as a complementary activity to the introduction of the Labour Code, consisting of Conventions on vocational training, co-operatives, labour administration and labour relations, social security, working conditions and the environment, and so on. At the beginning one could see ILO experts in countries helping the governments, trade unions and employers' associations to implement these Conventions and Recommendations. Of course, at a later stage (during the 1960s and 1970s) with the UN Development Programme (UNDP) taking up a much more important role, the ILO also entered other areas of technical assistance, with UNDP financing up to 60 per cent of all such activities.

Taken from a conventional ILO point of view, what would be the aspects of the organization's technical assistance activities which could be faulted? For example, in management development, one of the areas in which ILO technical assistance has been very active, the opportunity was missed by the ILO to use its experience to tackle some of the basic questions. Consider where most of the ILO experts come from: 16 per cent is from the UK, not exactly a country which is reputed for its pioneering work in management training; 6 per cent from the United States; The Netherlands 4 per cent; but Japan with some experience in this field provides only 0.3 per cent of ILO experts in this area. In rural development the technical assistance provided lacked focus, was too scattered, and when the ILO, in the early 1970s, tried to focus its rural development programme on the poverty approach, it was attacked by workers and employers alike. I shall come back to this latter issue.

However, from a conventional ILO point of view, some of the more interesting work in technical assistance has been done in the field of social security, because an attempt was made to determine to what extent developing countries can afford social security and welfare programmes at their level of development. In a way, it could be said that this was a very concrete way of tackling income distribution problems before it became fashionable. There are also certain activities in the ILO that have been declared 'holy' such as workers' education programmes, for example. Whatever happens in such areas will always be approved by the ILO Governing Body.

Walter Galenson, one of the US guardians of traditional ILO activities has concluded in a book entitled *The ILO, an American View*[2] that: 'In the traditional fields like vocational training, social security, occupational safety and health, ILO projects receive unanimous approbation. As soon as you move away from these specific and traditional fields, the record becomes much weaker: management development, small-scale industry, rural development. As soon as you start talking about really politically influenced projects imposed on the ILO by certain governments, you truly enter a disaster area'. There has always been a tendency for many influential people to say: 'ILO, stick to your specific labour problems in the narrow sense. If you do that, you also do good work for development at large'.

Despite these opinions, David Morse, who had been Director General of the ILO for more than 20 years, decided in 1969 to launch the World Employment Programme in order to get the ILO out of that straightjacket of specific industrial labour issues, to get it out of the modern sector, to get it out of organized labour and into the masses of the people. In short, to update the work of the organization.

The World Employment Programme

1969 was the 50th anniversary of the ILO and the Organization received the Nobel Prize for Peace in that year. At the same time The World Employment Programme was launched. A year later, David Morse who originated the idea of the WEP left! Even the Pope paid a visit in that memorable year 1969 and the following is a quote from his address to the Conference to the ILO. It is a quote concerning helping unemployed young people: 'Who has not sensed in the rich countries their [young unemployed people's] anxiety at the invasion of technocracy, their rejection of a society which has not succeeded in integrating them into itself? And in poor countries their lament that for lack of sufficient training and fitting means they cannot make their generous contribution to the tasks which call for it? In the present changing world their protest resounds like the cry of suffering and an appeal for justice'. Does that not sound very much like 1985? If you replace 'technocracy' – which was the May 1968 theme – by technology, for example, it is a very modern quote.

Standing on the broad shoulders of the mandate that was given to the ILO by the Declaration of Philadelphia, the World Employment Programme was comprehensive, covering all sectors of the economy, including all economic and social policies, population issues, income distribution and exchange rates. The main objectives of the World Employment Programme at the general level were then to reformulate economic and social development planning policies, within a comprehensive development strategy which would be more efficient in dealing with the problems of employment and income distribution. It was also to assist countries in implementing such strategies for which three means of action were created – comprehensive employment strategy missions, policy-oriented research programmes and country and regional employment teams. [3]

Employment then became for the ILO – in the broadest sense – a focus of economic and social development. In the very definition the ILO gave to the employment problem, it was shown that it went beyond the narrow labour definition. The new definition of the employment problem presented by the ILO focused on the income angle. Not only unemployment, but also over-employment (as was the case for many women in Africa) in which the workers were earning not more than a poverty return despite all their labour efforts, was included in the definition of the employment problem.

We developed the idea of the informal sector. We discussed the vicious circle of income distribution and employment creation, appropriate technology and education. In short, a broad sweep of problems was tackled during these years (the 1970s) by the World Employment Programme.

The conflict with the established ILO ideology was immediate, because we, in the World Employment Programme, were not very friendly towards the existing labour aristocracy, which was defended by organized labour represented in the ILO Governing Body and in the International Labour Conference. We proposed in several countries that those who were already employed in the modern sector should get less salary increases than anticipated, in favour of those who were not employed. This is a very topical discussion in OECD countries today. We attacked the ILO labour standards in the informal sector. It does not make sense to set marvellous standards for the informal sector as they may hinder development instead of stimulating it.

All this culminated in the 1976 World Employment Conference during which the concept of Basic Needs was launched. This concept was made rather controversial in spite of its being actually very close to conventional and narrowly defined ILO tradition and purposes. In a sense the World Employment Programme was also a symbol of the crisis in the United Nations. This will be discussed later.

The ILO Ideology and the Developing Countries

As I noted at the beginning, there are two ideologies within the ILO: the ideology of the structure of the organization and the ideology of the programme.[4] What exactly is the ideology of the structure? It is embedded in the constitutional provisions and the tripartite nature of the organization. In 1919 the battle-cry was liberal reformism, today it would probably be called social democratism. Anyway, in 1919 it was about liberal reformism and law. Law as an instrument of social engineering for reform and welfare in order to obtain incremental and reformist change; law as an instrument for balancing uneven social development and uneven power distribution – heavy emphasis was thus placed on the power of national law. This is the basis of the view that the passing of ILO Conventions into the domestic law of a nation would result in incremental change for social betterment. That was one important part of the ideology of the structure.

The second element was the belief in a plural society: workers and employers were seen as independent agents. In turn this was coupled with the belief that international meetings could settle internal affairs. It is very interesting to observe in this respect that the ILO would rather look at industrial safety and labour laws, that is internal conditions, than at multinationals and international trade which are international by nature. In the end it did look at these latter issues, of course, but it took some time to come to that.

The ideology of the structure is not necessarily the immediate and stated objective of an organization, but you cannot directly challenge the ideology of the structure without the organization changing its nature and its form. It is very basic.

The ideology of the programme is the part that is visible. It is generally described as THE ideology of THE organization. It depends on the fads and fashions of the day and on the personality of the Director General and his main deputies and staff. For example, the ILO was once seen as having an ideology of human resources development, of vocational training, of employment. In a way, that is the superstructure, but it is the ideology of the structure which is most important.

An example of the clashes between the two – and I have already hinted at them – is the case of the World Employment Programme. It is a pure demonstration of how these two ideologies clashed: the employed vis-à-vis the unemployed: the organized vis-à-vis the unorganized. The World Employment Programme research did not necessarily confirm that a plural society based on the vested interests of employers and workers was a good instrument for solving the problems of unemployment. We frequently had to say that organized labour was an obstacle to employment creation rather than an incentive.

In the first Governing Body meeting I attended as director of the WEP, I walked straight into the discussion about the Programme's mission report to Colombia. The Colombian trade unionist in the governing Body stood up and shouted that the report went against ILO traditions, that we had not talked sufficiently with the trade unions and that we had not even studied the Colombian Labour Code. He could not agree with what we proposed, because his members would be less well off than they would be if our recommendations were not implemented.

It has taken quite some time before the trade unions came around to the idea of putting some effort into organizing the unorganized. My impression is that in the end the ideology of the structure wins. The World Employment Programme, as far as I am concerned, has been absorbed into the main stream ideology. Although the trade unions did come some of the way.

In my archives I have some documents which provide some vivid illustrations of what I have just stated. I refer, for example, to an Evaluation Meeting of the World Employment Programme which took place after I left the ILO in December 1976. I was, of course, not invited. I received the following confidential information from a good friend of mine outside the organization. I quote: 'The relationship between the World Employment Programme and the other ILO activities was introduced by Mr X (Chief of the Bureau of Programme Budgeting and Management) and this led to a very emotional and controversial discussion. Mr X's thesis was that there was little relationship between the World Employment Programme work and that of the rest of the Organization; that the World Employment Programme has very much tended to work on its own; and that there was an underlying contradiction between the employment and basic needs approaches of the World Employment Programme and the traditional concerns of the ILO in the field of industrial relations, labour standards, etc. This theme was taken up even more vociferously by representatives of other units in the ILO, who attended that part of the discussion especially'.

Mr X today is the Director of the World Employment Programme. Although we are friends and I respect him it is clear to me that the old ILO, the entrenched trade unionists, the old-fashionedness, the selfishness in the end have won. Rigidity has won!

Under Attack: The ILO and the United Nations

The real problem of the ILO is illustrated by the well-known relationship between it and the United States which left the organization in 1976. It was not the US government that wanted to leave the organization, it was George Meany who for decades had been the dictator of the AFL–CIO and, believe me, only workers can be real dictators! Mr Meany did not like the way in which the Eastern European countries were treated in the ILO and of course he did not like the World Employment Programme. As soon as George Meany died, the United States rejoined the ILO.

Thus the real problem of the ILO is its tripartism which grants power to such narrow interests. It is like The Netherlands tripartite Socio-Economic Council (Sociaal-Economische Raad, SER) of which I have had some experience. It is of course interesting if policy-makers can talk, not only to governments but to workers and employers as well. But if these representatives really stick to their guns – their selfish and narrow standpoints – there is not much that can be done about the problems of employment, income distribution and basic needs. The ILO is a solid organization, but it is too rigid and the ideology of the structure is too rigid as well.

The World Employment Programme is in a sense a symbol for the crisis within the United Nations because (and in this respect the criticism was correct) it really should have been a programme undertaken by the UN proper. We, in the ILO had to co-ordinate all the other agencies – in fact, the United Nations should have done that, through the Economic and Social Council (ECOSOC) among other bodies.

The WEP was stepping into a vacuum that was created by the United Nations. The number two position in the United Nations, that of the Director General for International Co-operation and Development was in fact an attempt to create a post and attract a person who could co-ordinate the different agencies of the UN family involved with development problems. In reality it has been a reflection of the impotence of the United Nations.

Recently I had the occasion to spend about six weeks at the United Nations in New York dealing with a specific subject on which I was invited to report. I am sorry to say, there is still little vision and clout. At the same time, many specialized agencies are pathetic strongholds of selfish power. Their management styles are often pathetic. There is a big difference between having a forceful personality and having the vision and willpower to co-ordinate. The style of the people in charge is defensive with a strong tendency to run their empires like despots. There is dispersion and lack of co-ordination, which is a reflection of national disorder in dealing with the United Nations. The different national ministries all have exclusive lines to their appropriate UN agencies.

It seems there is no thought given to the future of technical assistance and no thinking about the role of the UN Development Programme (UNDP). I know this, because at the Institute of Social Studies for five years we have organized seminars for UNDP Resident Representatives. There is no forward-thinking towards the 'next problem'. There is no UN view, for example, on a subject like adjustment policies as opposed to the IMF point of view. There continues to be the situation in which one country is allowed to pay 25 per cent of the budget of the organization. It is a ridiculous situation. How can the other countries allow one single country to pay 25 per cent of the budget enabling it to throw its weight around? Nothing is being done about that situation.

Conclusions

1. The UN organization proper and the specialized agencies are becoming old and rigid bureaucracies.

2. There is too much political influence involved when it comes to appointments. It should be possible to oppose that.
3. There is too much influence by the United States because of the budgetary structure.
4. There is no vision, just muddling along well-trodden paths. ILO is not even the worst of the UN system. It has at least a very original instrument of action in the Conventions. The ILO must adapt its Conventions more to the growing heterogeneity of the world – more than it has done so far.

Notes

1) The problems surrounding the identification of a minimum package which could be universally applied are discussed in: (Dutch) National Advisory Council for Development Co-operation, *Recommendation on Minimum International Labour Standard*, The Hague, 1984, no. 84.

2) Walter Galenson, *The International Labour Organization: An American View*, University of Wisconsin Press, Madison, 1981.

3) See L. Emmerij, 'Introduction: The World Employment Programme', in: Willy van Ryckeghem (ed.), *Employment Problems and Policies in Developing Countries*, Rotterdam University Press, Rotterdam, 1976.

4) See J. Harrod, 'The Ideology of the International Labour Organization towards Developing Countries', in: *The Impact of International Organizations on Legal and Institutional Change in Developing Countries*. International Legal Centre, New York, 1977, pp. 184–210.

9 UNESCO: Structural Origins of Crisis and Needed Reforms

Maarten Mourik*

Introduction

The following analysis of the problems of the United Nations Educational, Scientific and Cultural Organization (UNESCO) is based on my long official relationship with the organization and a thorough knowledge of its workings. However, the views expressed here, and especially those relating to the remedies for the current problems of UNESCO are given in my personal capacity and are not necessarily shared by my government.

UNESCO is not at the moment the most respected of organizations within the UN system, at least not in Western Europe, and although, therefore, I do not intend to be laudatory about it I hope to be able to point to some specific ways whereby it could regain respectability.

In this chapter, then, I will argue that many of the current difficulties of UNESCO today are the result of ideas incorporated in its constitutional structure at the beginning and that only an understanding of these structural faults and their necessary repair will offer any viable solution.

* *Maarten Mourik* is Ambassador for International Cultural Relations at the Dutch Ministry of Foreign Affairs. He was The Netherlands Ambassador to UNESCO between 1978 and 1985, prior to which he was deputy chief of mission of The Netherlands delegation to the OECD, Paris. He has published a large number of articles on international affairs and seven volumes of poetry.

I begin with a quote: 'All organizations need regular, frank and fair criticism. The United Nations Educational, Scientific and Cultural Organization... does not get enough of that. One of its great weaknesses is over-defensiveness, unwillingness to listen to criticism. This lesson – of the value of open, critical comment – is one UNESCO really must learn or it will become even more of an enclosed Byzantine system than it is at present'.

These words are found in the preface to one of the best books that was ever written about UNESCO. Its title is *An Idea and its Servants: UNESCO from Within* (London, Chatto & Windus 1978). It was published nine years ago. Its knowledgeable author was a British former Assistant Director-General, Richard Hoggart. It seems worthwhile noting that Mr Hoggart did not serve under the present Director-General of UNESCO but under his predecessor, René Maheu of France. Here is another pertinent quotation from the same work: 'The burden of this book is, that, in spite of all the weaknesses which I describe, UNESCO is still an immensely valuable organization. I believe it is a sick organization at present, for a number of reasons which involve all those concerned with it – member States, the international non-governmental organizations, the world intellectual community as a whole and the "Secretariat" (p. 23).

Mr Hoggart's call for 'regular, frank and fair criticism' seems to have been more than met in recent years, although some observers feel that such criticism has been less than fair and that UNESCO has been made the scapegoat for all the sins of the UN system as a whole, in particular by its Western members.

I am not sure that at the moment 'UNESCO is still an immensely valuable organization' as Hoggart puts it. The sickness of which he spoke has since then turned out to be a chronic malignant malady with many metastases, paralysing a considerable number of sub-organs. But how serious the state of its health may be, the organization can still be operated upon, in which event those responsible may heed an old Dutch saying: 'Faint-hearted surgeons allow wounds to fester'.

Continuing within the domain of medical metaphors, I would like to present my main theme, which is that most of UNESCO's present day difficulties are caused by birth defects. This realization has profound implications because it presupposes basic surgery before UNESCO will be able to lead a more normal life.

In this case history of UNESCO an endeavour will be made to distinguish between what I consider to be fundamental or structural problems and a dense and often parasitical overgrowth of incidental difficulties, difficulties that are in many instances more of a personal than a factual nature.

UNESCO Constitution: A Hybrid Structure

UNESCO's founding conference took place in London in November, 1945 and its Constitution came into force a year later, when 20 member States had joined. I would like to emphasize this figure: 20 members.

Two basically conflicting mainstreams of thought found their way into UNESCO's constitution. As a result the constitution which emerged has a hybrid character which is responsible for most of the organization's current problems. The first basic idea was that of a rather independent organization consisting of eminent personalities from the worlds of science, education and the arts modelled to a certain degree on the pre-war Paris-based International Institute for Intellectual Co-operation. This institute had an affiliation with the League of Nations. Einstein and Freud were among its members.

Such an organization being free of government and State would of course have a high degree of independence and objectivity, but as the history of the International Institute for Intellectual Co-operation had shown, its dealings would have little or no impact upon the policies of the countries represented. Lack of funding would also impede its activities.

It was mainly for these latter reasons that the founding fathers, although not altogether rejecting this model, established an intergovernmental organization. This had the obvious drawback of being liable to direct political influences and pressures from the side of member States' governments, but, conversely, would offer greater opportunities for the ideas and proposals accepted within the organization to be brought to the attention of policy planners and political decision-makers in member countries. Movement in the opposite direction would be equally secured, namely exchanges of ideas between governments and the secretariat of the organization.

The idea of independent international intellectual co-operation, as embodied in the former Paris institute, was not lost altogether. It was reflected in the creation of National Commissions, to be composed of eminent representatives in the fields of competence of UNESCO. These representatives, acting as advisors to their governments, were to guarantee the high standard of national intellectual input. Wider interests, regional or even international, were to be safeguarded by the affiliation of a large number of international professional non-governmental organizations, now commonly called NGOs. In addition, and most importantly, an Executive Board was established. Its seats were to be distributed on a geographical basis, its members to be nominated à titre privé, that is not in the first place as representatives of their governments, but because of their eminent qualities in one or more of UNESCO's domains. This body was to monitor the organization's activities on a regular basis through two half-yearly sessions of approximately five weeks' work.

Obviously, this was a construction with a precarious balance which could be easily disturbed. Even in the days before UNESCO's birth it was clear to most people involved that the greatest risk of disturbance of this balance would come from governments which would let political interests prevail over the interests of international intellectual co-operation.

In order to counterbalance this risk of politicization as far as possible, it was thought desirable to invest the Executive of the organization – the Director-General – with a high degree of autonomous power. This provision is at the hub of UNESCO's problems, although on the surface of things this seemed to be a reasonable solution. Take for example, the Constitutional mandate of the Director-General which is 'to prepare for submission to the Board a draft programme of work for the Organization with corresponding budget estimates' (UNESCO Constitution 1946 Art. VI. 3a). Another example: he is authorized to 'appoint the staff of the Secretariat in accordance with staff regulations to be approved by the General Conference'. (Art. VI.4). Nothing seems to be wrong here, provided that:

1. The Director-General tries to divide his attention evenly amongst the manifold interests represented in the organization, and
2. Governments, forming together the legislative branch of the organization, are able and willing to exert the necessary controls over the Executive, that is, the Director-General.

The situation at the time of the creation of UNESCO could be summarized as follows:

1. A composite legislative body (the collective membership) with a relatively heavy political and an equally weak cultural component ('cultural' being used in the broadest sense of the word).
2. An executive arm (the Director-General and his secretariat) given extensive powers to enable it, as far as possible, to shield the cultural interests of the organization from politicization.

In order to judge this construction fairly it is necessary to recall the political and spiritual climate surrounding UNESCO's birth: politically there prevailed amongst the victors of World War II the postwar euphoria on international co-operation in general, while the *spiritual* setting was still characterized mainly by the belief that education would improve people and that more knowledge of each other would automatically lead to a better understanding and, therefore, a better relationship between the nations of this world. These ideas can be traced back to the Age of Enlightenment and its humanistic ideals.

The Development of Politicization in UNESCO

In a static world this structure might have functioned reasonably well, as it did for nearly a decade. But the post-World War II world was far from static. First there were the latent tensions between East and West which very soon turned into a 'cold war'. No less important in its consequences for the world as a whole and for UNESCO in particular, was the process of decolonization. The latter resulted in an explosive growth of UN membership, including that of UNESCO, which now has more than 160 members. Given the absence in UNESCO of a veto power for the larger members, this meant that within two decades the majority position of the West was transformed into an uneasy minority position.

Such a fall from power would undoubtedly have been digested with less discomfort if the new minority had not remained as a paying majority. This aspect too, should be taken into account when evaluating UNESCO's present crisis.

Cold war and decolonization had important implications for UNESCO's political climate: East found itself pitted against West, North against South. This of course is a simplification of existing relations but the overall result for UNESCO's members was an absolute lack of coherence of policies, of common views, of any prevailing vision at all. Politicization became general. In other words, the legislative arm of the organization, unable to organize itself, lost most of its power. Many political scientists consider it a natural law that whenever there is a power vacuum it will be filled one way or another – at UNESCO it was filled by the Director-General.

Politicization on a general scale, as described above, was reinforced within UNESCO by two subsidiary developments which were both results and further causes of politicization. The first one was the 'de-culturisation' of the Executive Board. Governments, vaguely or more acutely, feeling their grip on things at UNESCO loosening, became less and less inclined to send delegates to the Executive Board who could also speak for themselves and, therefore, would not have necessarily represented only official views. Today the Board member who is not in the first instance a political nominee is rare indeed. It is hardly necessary to say that this, too, fostered politicization.

Secondly, politicization brought with it the elimination of the initial dynasty of Directors-General, whose first member was Julian Huxley succeeded by Torres Bodet and Luther Evans. Particularly the first two Directors-General were outstanding people in the scientific and cultural field. Evans was not quite their peer but administered the organization better. He failed however to secure it from the inroads of McCarthyism when he allowed staff members to appear before the United States House Un-American Activities Committee and thereby compromised the supra-national status of international civil servants. With René Maheu there entered a new breed of Directors-General, no longer outstanding scholars or distinguished writers, but rather technocrats – technocrats with a strong political sense.

The Directors-General and Personal Rule

The new breed of Directors-General way of running the organization became a very personal one. In a global organization which not only lacks controlling power, but where those who should exercise this power are hopelessly divided among themselves, for he who is bent on power there are hardly any limits. Hardly any limits to setting groups against each other, to exercising an absolutely personal staff policy, to concealing the relationship between resources and activities, to disconnecting the establishment of the two-yearly programme and its execution. Hardly any limits to pushing through one's own ideas when a medium-term plan had to be established. Autocratic behaviour moreover leads to isolation, to Byzantine conditions where the courtier and the court-jester are more valued than the honest worker.

I have on purpose not burdened the discourse with lists of facts and figures. At present I stand somewhat apart from the daily chores of UNESCO which well enables me to follow the secular lines of development. I have, therefore, refrained from going into the main political, managerial and administrative controversies within UNESCO, because I consider them to be surface phenomena of deeper-rooted problems. Once these problems are solved, most of the secondary difficulties will also disappear. This goes for questions like the New World Information and Communication Order (NWICO), that of human rights versus peoples' rights and for the hardy perennials of peace and disarmament. This does not mean that these secondary problems would not be responsible for the poisoning of many relationships among members and between members and the secretariat.

To quote Hoggart once more, at the point where he takes stock of Maheu's term of office: 'But overall he left an Organization too centrally run, too much urged on by fear, internally, and by political manoeuvrings in its external relations. He left an Organization far too short on inner courage, and so all the more open to the even greater politicization which now threatens it.' (p. 155)

The Insufficiency of Partial Reforms

The above quote from Hoggart was written more than nine years ago and things have become worse since then. No wonder that United States' withdrawal from UNESCO, announced by the end of 1983 and carried out in December, 1984, came as both a heavy blow and as a salutary shock at the same time. The threat of withdrawal set into motion a reform movement, led by the group of Western members, with the rather passive consent of the United States. Not much was obtained in the way of reforms during 1984, at least too little to convince the United States that it should stay on or the United Kingdom not to withdraw which it did in 1985. Unfortunately, the US departure from the UNESCO scene virtually stopped the reform movement. In my view continued US membership could have opened up possibilities for further reforms, maybe even for fundamental changes which now seem out of reach for years to come. Since then UNESCO's membership has had to put up a bitter fight all through this year, just to safeguard the meagre reform results of the year before. Maybe some skirmishes were won, but there has been no victory in a real battle, let alone a war. Therefore, I fail to see any basic positive element in the most recent developments.

At this time when important decisions need to be taken, the meeker position is to argue to stay in and work for reforms from the inside. But when the house is crumbling and on the verge of collapsing, it is not sufficient just to plaster over the cracks in the walls and put fresh paint on the rotten beams. One has to renovate both the whole infrastructure and superstructure as well.

In practice such renovation would mean a number of constitutional changes which would put real responsibility for programming and medium-term planning with the bodies representing member States. Present procedures make a farce of this responsibility most of the time. Further constitutional reforms would have to strengthen the role of National Commissions and NGOs in programming, would have to strengthen the principle of consensus in matters important to all members and would have to limit the discretionary powers of the Director-General in personnel matters. Finally, real budgetary clarity and detailed independent auditing, should be established.

I find it regrettable that none of the Western countries has even come close to making any of these proposals, although they should be aware of the fact that the universality of UNESCO, or, in other words, the return of the United States, depends upon their implementation.

In the past, Western countries have waited far too long before taking a stand against the disintegration of UNESCO. Stemming that process of disintegration is not enough. If UNESCO is to have a future, and it certainly deserves one, member countries should not timidly stop short. It requires courage to take unpopular initiatives, to question vested interests both at home and within the organization. But then, again: 'Faint-hearted surgeons allow wounds to fester'.

10 United Nations Specialized Agencies: From Functionalist Intervention to International Co-operation?

Jeffrey Harrod*

In this chapter I will develop some comments and arguments concerning the past and emerging roles of the main specialized agencies of the United Nations which deal with social issues. While I will concentrate principally on the four UN agencies normally most associated with social activities, namely the World Health Organization (WHO), International Labour Organization (ILO), the UN Educational, Scientific and Cultural Organization (UNESCO) and the UN Food and Agricultural Organization (FAO), all international organizations, both governmental and inter-governmental, have been to some extent subject to the shifts in roles that I will identify.

Perhaps the underlying interest is to consider the place of international organization in relation to the integrated regimes of intellectual, professional and political concerns which affect and infect perceptions of the world, consciousness of its dynamics and, in consequence, the political actions in relation to it. International organization as a global mirror of these regimes, as a global instrument of their perpetuation and as a marginal commentator on their fragility has been a crucial element in the development of the 20th century world and its intellectual discourses. In this view, international organization represents the sole global link to any global consciousness; it is within this context that I

* *Jeffrey Harrod* is a writer on international social and economic affairs and Professor Extraordinary at the Institute of Social Studies, The Hague. Between 1969 and 1973 he worked at the International Institute of Labour Studies/ILO. He has published widely in the fields of international organization, foreign policy, international political economy and international labour conditions.

more mundanely take up the discussion of the UN social activities and the organizations associated with them.

UN Social and Economic Activities: Some Orders of Magnitude

The UN social and economic activities can be seen to be undertaken by forms of organizations along a line which starts from the more traditional 'membership-fee' organizations and ends in the 'fund' type of organizations. As with all such constructs, in the middle of the line is a penumbra in which the two forms merge.

The 'fund' organizations are those set up around special funds donated by various states to the United Nations as an executing agency. The United Nations then sets up a secretariat to administer the use of the funds. The most well-known examples of these are the UN International Children's Emergency Fund (UNICEF), the UN Fund for Population Activities (UNFPA) and the UN High Commissioner for Refugees (UNHCR).

The 'membership-fee' organizations are those in which a member state pays a fee for membership to be disbursed by an independent secretariat – these then basically become independent organizations associated with the United Nations and for the most part they are the 'specialized agencies' of the UN system.

Most of the UN specialized agencies were created in their current form between 1944–1949. This was a process of new creation, such as in the cases of the FAO and UNESCO, or of reformulation and restructuring, such as in the cases of the ILO (which was in fact founded in 1919) and the Universal Postal Union (founded in 1878). In this process some anomalies emerged. The agencies specifically charged with the possibility of global economic management were not only given constitutions which differed from the mainstream social, cultural and technical agencies, they were also incorporated into the UN system in a different way: thus the so-called Bretton Woods institutions – the International Monetary Fund (IMF) and the International Bank for Reconstruction and Development (IBRD or World Bank) were never part of the UN system in the same manner as, for example, the WHO. Indeed, in the case of the World Bank elements of its constitution, particularly Article II paragraph (ii) of the Articles of Agreement which states that the purpose of the organization is 'to promote private foreign investment', departed so far from the notion of universality as to prevent full participation by all states with different socio-economic systems.

Apart from these Bretton Woods organizations the UN agencies dealing with social and technical issues may be divided into two categories – the agencies with a technical mandate and which also have a fee-based expenditure of less than $100 million and the social and economic organizations which have budgets of over $100 million. In the first category are organizations such as the World Meteorological Organization (WMO) with a regular budget of $19.1 million and the International Telecommunications Union (ITU) with a regular budget of

$51.1 million. In the second category there are really only four organizations of importance, the ILO with a regular budget of $127 million, the FAO with $210 million, the UNESCO with $210 million and WHO with $260 million. The smaller technical agencies employ between 159 persons in the case of the Universal Postal Union (UPU) to over 1000 persons for the International Civil Aviation Organization (ICAO), while for the larger social and economic agencies employment figures range between nearly 3000 for the ILO to nearly 7000 for the FAO.[1]

Before preceding further it is important to put the size of the budgets and staff of these organizations into some quantitative perspective. The budget expenditures of the organizations are divided into two parts – the regular budget derived from members' fees and the funds which come from other sources, often from pledging conferences and other entities of the UN system such as the United Nations Development Programme (UNDP). The combination of the regular and extra budget items can be considered as the organizations' turnover or cash flow. In 1984, the total of the regular budgets for the 11 agencies with a technological and socio-economic mandate was just over $1 billion and the total cash flow was almost exactly $2 billion. The total employment for the 11 agencies was 23 thousand persons.

These are extremely modest figures. $2 billion as the total turnover for the whole 11 organizations is less than 1/7 of the turnover for one single multi-national company, such as that of the Bayer Corporation, which had a $14 billion turnover in 1984 and employed some 200 thousand people. $2 billion is less than 1/3 of the budget of the single city of New York.

The four agencies of special concern in this chapter – ILO, FAO, WHO and UNESCO – spend about $1.5 billion and employ 18 thousand people. That these agencies are so widely discussed, that their output is integrated into the regimes of professional concerns, that there is a body of theoretical literature about them, that their initials and symbols are known by every professional within their field of operation and that large sections of the world population are also familiar with them surely must already be a hallmark of success – the success of making a little go a long way.

Despite these undeniable impacts made on policy discussions and secured with slender funds it is precisely these organizations which have recently come under attack in a manner and to an extent unique in their history. In particular, they are castigated for their superfluity and 'inefficiency'. All confrontations of this sort are combinations of new criticisms and the decay of old defences and it is for the latter reason that it is important to consider the past rationales for the founding and existence of the agencies dealing with socio-economic issues.

Rationales for UN Socio-economic Activities

The socio-economic activities of the United Nations embodied in the specialized agencies have been supported by four basic arguments. These are: first, the

World State objective; second, the realist perspective in international relations; third, the liberal-internationalists' orientation; and fourth, the functionalist theory of peace and integration. In this section each of these is taken in turn to examine its fortunes over the 40 years of UN history.

The idea that humanity and the UN system should agitate towards the creation of a World State may seem far-fetched today. But this idea was certainly around at the founding of the United Nations and the specialized agencies were certainly part of the grand scheme. Thus Francis Wilcox, Assistant Secretary of State (United States) for International Organization, sought to assure a US House of Representatives Committee even in 1953 that the specialized agencies 'do not constitute a world government nor do they in any way represent a threat to our sovereignty'.[2] Even if the objective of a World State itself was rarely made explicit there were certainly notions in the early days of a global society and the development of a universal culture. These ideas were almost completely abandoned by the late 1950s although the remaining structure in organogramic forms still does produce the impression that the ILO, WHO, UNESCO and FAO are the embryonic world ministries of Labour, Health, Education and Agriculture.

It may seem surprising that the realist perception – that is that international relations are governed exclusively by attempts to maximize power to the exclusion of morality and ethics – could be used in support of the specialized agencies. But once it became clear that the idealism in the constitutions of the agencies was not considered as a viable proposition for execution and would not necessarily be a guiding principle of action, then the agencies could indeed be seen as useful instruments for the maximization of power at the international level. To quote Wilcox again, 'but finally and from the point of view of our own national interest and our own foreign policy, the specialized agencies assume great significance as channels through which we can meet the Soviet challenge'.[3] The realist argument is still used within separate nation states to defend both the existence of the agencies and the principle of universality of membership on the grounds that power is maximized by staying in rather than pulling out or closing down. It is the challenge to the proposition – that power is indeed maximized by staying in – that has recently shaken the habits of two decades of international diplomatic practice.

The liberal-internationalist, perhaps the oldest and the most romantic strain of thought and attitude which supports international organization postulates that international co-operation is an ideal and an expression of the basic sameness of the human condition despite the differences of language, culture and race. The liberal-internationalist perception was strong after the Second World War and international organization, as a subject to be taught at universities and as the basis for a theory of peace, gathered a strong army of supporters. But these supporters suffered greatly during the early part of the Cold War when they were often branded as idealists easily duped in a hard world of power and disguised enemies. But this was not the only cause of the weakness of this body of support

– the raw experiences of international work and contact in which it was soon discovered that ideals of common brotherhood and sisterhood of humankind were not universally shared and that part of the human condition is also pettiness, viciousness and hypnotism with status, promotion and personal power, soured the liberal internationalists who came into contact with it. Indeed there is ample evidence that holders of such ideas are entirely unsuited to international service. When their cherished ideas are confronted with reality the result is a violent rejection of the ideal and a retreat into theories of national inequalities and the hopelessness of other cultures, races and persons. Nevertheless, for the purposes of the review here, it can be said with certainty that liberal-internationalist support has weakened and is weakened even more as stories of corruption and self-seeking within international organization proliferate.

The functional thesis of international organization is the fourth argument in favour and support of the UN agencies and it has been the most successful. For this latter reason it will be dealt with at greater length.

The functional thesis as it comes down to us from its now recognized founding father, David Mitrany, was that world integration and therefore world peace would be constructed by two basic mechanisms, first, that international co-operation and then integration would be secured by concentrating on so-called non-political tasks within universal human environments – such as improvement of labour conditions, increased food production and so on. Second, that the experience of international service would cause people to see its superior virtue over that of national service and that firm transnational social, economic and technical linkages would be made which would eventually confound the linkages made by statement and summit conferences. In short, Mitrany was saying 'the more they know each other the more they love each other', in opposition to the Von Clausewitz aphorism expounded in his work on war which was, 'the more they know each other the more they hate each other'.

Within the Mitrany concept of functionalism there was a demon and a hero. The demon was the politician or statesman. Politics divided the world and the state stifled natural transborder activities. For Mitrany 'our social activities are cut off arbitrarily at the limit of the state and, if at all, are allowed to be linked to the same activities across the borders only by means of uncertain and cramping political ligatures'.[4] The state was then the dominator and destructor of a more peaceful world. The hero was the expert – scientists were value-free, rational and pursued efficiency and progress – in contrast with the statesmen who pursued power and were nationalist. To the Mitrany functionalism the neo-functionalists added the vague notion of integration proceeding by an individual transfer of loyalty from the nation state to the material benefit-supplying international entity.

This theory provided powerful support for the founding of the specialized agencies. They were functional, concentrating in a specific area, they proceeded by co-operation based on experts, and they were international. Thus even in

1980, after considering the failures and difficulties of 'functionalist' learning in international co-operation, a researcher notes that it is still in the world at large a most potent prescriptive device 'for more international co-operation with appropriate institutionalization in areas of recognized need.'[5]

The remainder of this chapter must consider first, what happened to the functionalist idea in practice and second, does the last quoted statement still hold its intellectual force, and if not, what other arguments can be brought to the defense of the specialized agencies?

Periods in the UN Social Affairs Experience

The history of the specialized agencies can be divided into three periods which might be termed the periods of limited international co-operation, the period of functionalist intervention, and the period of hegemony.

The period of *limited international co-operation* can be seen as being roughly between the emergence of the current structure of the agencies, say 1944–47 through to the mid 1950s. The reason why the international co-operation was 'limited' was because during this time there were only a few member States and they were mostly the States of Europe and North America. The reason why the period expresses 'co-operation' and not functional integration was that these member States in practice rejected the theory because of their reluctance to accept the political effects of it.

Inherent in the functionalist thesis is a strong anti-State idea which is one reason for the importance of non-governmental organizations in the theory. In fact the UN agencies were, according to the theory, to be subversive to the State, attacking its power by the promotion of equally powerful and effective transnational activities.

But the agencies were launched amongst state members at a time when the State had never been more powerful. Since Keynes' dictum that the State was responsible for full employment the nation States in post-war Europe were building welfare-states at great speed; never before in the history of humankind have citizens more reason to look to the State and adhere to the nation State for now it was not only for reasons of emotive nationalism but also for reasons of direct material benefits. As Wilcox noted there was no chance that any sovereignty from this apparatus would be surrendered nor were the States prepared to allow their rather new ministries of labour, health and so on to be influenced by foreign 'experts'.

What happened then was that the agencies – judging from a newspaper search made of the period 1947–1956 of the English language newspapers (principally The Times and New York Times) – concentrated on issues which were international by nature. This meant, for example, transmissible diseases in the case of WHO, internationally-based industries such as shipping in the case of the ILO, and compilations of international statistics and handbooks.

The period of *functionalist intervention* ranges from the end of the 1950s to at least the mid-1970s. Had it not been for the emergence of what are now called the third world States the functionalist thesis in practice might have been stillborn. The emergence into the international scene beginning in the late 1950s of the new, weak third world States provided a golden opportunity for the attempted operationalization of the functionalist thesis, here was room for the 'international expert', here were populations not yet imbued with the pro-State virus so much believed to be the case in Europe and elsewhere, here was the possibility, for example, of the WHO developing a parallel loyalty to that of the nation State for its role in the eradication of malaria and other such diseases.

But, of course, here was the opportunity for the ex-colonial powers and the new neo-colonial powers to find 'legitimate' and palatable channels with which to continue to influence, if not govern, the ex-colonies from a distance. It was also the opportunity to attempt to preserve a 'pluralism' in the new States, to strengthen non-governmental organizations and so keep open, permeable societies in which there was access – access for capital, to raw materials and for vacationers. To quote Wilcox again speaking at the beginning of this period: 'In closing I would like to quote a statement of Laird Bell, distinguished lawyer and chairman of the Weyerhaeser Timber Co. Mr Bell was one of our delegates at the last UN General Assembly. Speaking of the UN technical assistance and agricultural assistance to Africa, Southeast Asia and South America he said: 'I doubt that any dollars we spend are better spent than on that assistance. My own feeling is that it is justification enough for the UN".[6]

It was no accident then that in this period, of the 1200 experts sent to the developing countries by the ILO, 500 were British and 450 were French. International experts tended to be ex-colonial administrators; thus in a technical assistance report of the ILO in 1949 it is stated 'the expert chosen for this mission, Sir Malcom Darling of Great Britain, chairman of the Horace Plunkett Foundation has had some 35 years' experience working with agriculturalists in the Punjab'.[7]

But there was a contradiction. The objective of most newly independent States was precisely a) to mobilise the people for development or other political objectives, b) to strengthen the power and competence of the State. This is why, writing at the end of this period in 1974 I noted that the functionalist notions inherent in the specialized agency operations meant that 'functional transnationalism is pitted against mobilising nationalism.'[8] Functionalism became the intellectual and practical vehicle for an attempted moulding of the new States into pluralist, permeable States open to all influences and penetrations which by the nature of the world would originate in the ex-metropolitan and more powerful States.

The period of *hegemony* – roughly from the mid-1970s to the early 1980s – saw the contradiction between transnational functionalism and mobilising nationalism resolved in favour of the latter. In the 20 years between 1955 and 1975 a transformation of the world political scene had taken place. It was not just the formal appearance of over 80 new States but, far more important, the speed with which the national strength and competence of these States developed. In a very short space of time the new States developed technically and administratively competent personnel with high professional standards and devotion to duty. Contrary to the Mitrany idea, it was the experts in the *service* of the State who stood in contrast to the politicians, the latter being often directly or indirectly in the service of one or other of the great powers. The development of the competence and extension of the State in third world countries was rapid and definitive. The result of this was that the new States began to react like the old ones; they began to reject the exhortations of the international expert, reject development projects designed in metropolitan centres to be executed in ex-colonial hinterlands, reject personnel whose main claim to expertise was to have been prised from their colonial enclaves by wars of national independence.

Even as the internal strength of the new States was gathering other changes in the environment were taking place: the first rich ex-developing countries – the oil-exporting States and newly industrialising States – appeared, long-haul air travel shortened operational and administrative distances, the extent and influence of multinational corporations and integrated international production rapidly increased.

After a period of direct world government through empire, of indirect government through economic pressure there now emerged a world governance founded on hegemony. Hegemony is the form of government based on securing an acceptance amongst the lowest in the hierarchy of the ideas and perceptions which suit the purposes of the highest in the hierarchy. One of the first steps in the construction of such a hegemony was to establish a globalisation of professional discourse: thus this was the period of global conferences and 'one-world' global reports, of which 'The Limits to Growth' by the Club of Rome was a notable example, and of the global conferences on such issues as food, population, human rights and environment. The emerging global professional discourse was to be actualized by UN agencies in a manner which indicated their role in a hegemonic system: the major programmes not only reflected but also promoted the ideas and perceptions necessary to sustain a basic continuity of the *status quo*.

Examples of these latter programmes may be given but it is best to do so in the next section and in contrast to what is replacing them in the most recent times. These events cannot yet be seen as a specific period in which there can be a designated end. Rather the beginning can be seen as the weakening of hegemony but the end has yet to be resolved.

From Hegemony to Universal International Co-operation?

The hegemonic period is still with us but its dominance and its peak were relatively short-lived. It began to show cracks in the early 1980s which opened into fissures by the mid 1980s. One of the causes of this was the growing intellectual excellence, professional competence and expertise within the third world. One of the contradictions of all imperialism and hegemony is the need to educate the operatives for the continued support of the system but such education at the same time provokes investigative thought and more simply the questioning of orders and ideas received. Third world intellectuals and professionals moved from reactive defense to positive action. The reactive defense being the questioning of the competence, ideas and panaceas promoted by the international system and the positive action, the actual replacement of the old experts and ideas by those more fitted to the real needs of the lowest in the rung of the world hierarchy – in short the beginning of the end of hegemony.

The impact on the social agencies of the UN has been a profound and radical rupture with past modes of operation. The most well-known aspect of this is, of course, the voting strength of the third world in the agencies. This strength enabled the rejection of hegemonic programmes and the provision of finance for others. But it is a mistake to believe, as it is often said, that the irritation of the major financing countries of Western Europe and North America – the so-called 'Geneva Group' – is over the ability of the majority to vote to spend more and more money in their favour. It was not the *amount* of money that was to be spent as much as *how* it was to be spent. The irritation, in fact, stemmed from the increasingly anti-hegemonic research, publication and policies of the organizations.

The first manifestation of the nature of future programmes appeared formally in the promulgation of highly idealist and rather abstract declarations of 'new orders'. Thus throughout the 1970s each agency formulated, adopted or associated itself with new order programmes – The New International Economic Order of the UN General Assembly and UNCTAD, the New World Information and Communication Order of UNESCO, The Health for All Programme of the WHO, and an updated World Employment Programme for the ILO are such examples.

Despite their often abstract nature these new programmes in fact meant a fundamental change in what can be called the organizational ideology. To give but two examples. In the case of the ILO the organization had throughout its history insisted that what should be promoted amongst the member States was the so-called voluntary settlement of labour disputes rather than judicial settlement. This was a direct result of the original and continuing British influence in the organization. But developing countries often with a surfeit of lawyers, ironically the result of law being the preferred subject to train the colonized in democracy, wished to install judicial settlement procedures. For many years the organization would not provide technical assistance for the development of judicial settlement. The end of hegemony meant the end of such orientations in programmes. In the case of the WHO, for many years the organization had been prevented from offering technical assistance for the creation of para-medical personnel largely through the influence of national associations of doctors, such as the American Medical Association (AMA). These associations, pursuing a trade union restrictive practices policy as they had done domestically, insisted within the WHO that all medical assistance must be given by, or in the presence of, a fully qualified doctor. There is no need to elaborate how this policy retarded the development of effective primary health care based on para-medical personnel in many countries of the third world. This policy was finally broken in the mid 1970s when the organization received the mandate to promote officially the use of para-medical personnel in health care. Other issues of similar nature concerned the use of generic name drugs and the development of public and preventive health programmes which have brought the organization recently into conflict with the world pharmaceutical, infant food, and now the tobacco and alcohol industries.[9]

Changes occurred in the research and publications of the organizations which also incurred the wrath of dominant powers. During the functional intervention phase publications were often prepared by experts on observation missions – very similar in fact to the 'go and appreciate' mandate of colonial investigation officers. During the hegemonic period the practice was what might be called 'consensus' publication which was that every word had to be vetted to ensure that no member State was offended by it. This meant of course that there could be no challenge to the fundamental ideology of the organization given that such ideologies were similar if not identical to those of the dominant powers. It also meant a generalized heightened sense of sovereignty, the Article 2, paragraph 7 of the UN Charter mentality. For example, a statistic and its publication is the sovereign property of a member State. Thus, if a State claims it has a 90 per cent literacy rate but independent studies show it has only a 50 per cent literacy rate, then the official statistic must prevail in official international publications.

In the post-hegemonic phase what seems to have happened is that there is a majority acceptance of two fundamental principles. First, a form of non-reciprocal tolerance has emerged among third world countries concerning publications which show certain aspects of their societies in an unfavourable light. Thus State X will not protest about a study of the exploitation of child workers within its boundaries provided the same organization also makes a study of prostitutes in State Y. The result is that over the past few years the publications of the UN social activity agencies have had some value in the political world; they have finally started to supply real and pertinent information.[10]

Second, publications which supply evidence for the destruction of hegemonic myths are generally accepted by the majority of States. On the other hand the power of the promotors of such myths is now not always sufficient to prevent publication, as happened in the past with ILO studies of national income distribution and more recently the WHO studies on the alcohol industry.

The most instructive evidence in support of these two above observations is the forms and nature of the opposition to publications and other activities in support of the new order programmes. In the case of the WHO an attempt to monitor and enforce by publication a code of conduct designed to mitigate bad effects from the advertising of infant food in the third world in the face of the opposition of several multinational companies, the tactics included attacks on the organizations, its delegates and supporters in various journals; in one case the Nestlé company paid $25,000 to a writer to publish such an attack without attribution in *Fortune* magazine.[11] Significantly when leaving UNESCO in protest of its inefficiency the British government called for *less* publication and research and *more* in-field technical assistance activities.

The 'new-order' programmes not only spawned anti-hegemonic publications and research but also the only real form of action any international organization could take in support of proposed changes in the processes by which the world is governed – the formulation, promulgation and monitoring of codes of practice and conduct. 'Codes' then proliferated in much the same manner as 'new orders' – the GATT commercial code, the UNCTAD code on restrictive business practices, the WHO code on infant food advertising, the UNESCO code on journalist practices and so on.[12] When codes of conduct are constructed to enforce conformity to a myth which is widely upheld but in practice widely ignored, (such as that of free trade, business competition, respect for human rights, subsidiary autonomy, or unbiased newspaper reporting) or try to establish new forms of behaviour then they are on a collision course with 'established practices'. In short, they are on a collision course with the practices cemented by hegemony into the *status quo*.

New orders, research and publication in support of them, and codes of conduct brought accusations against the organizations as being nothing more than 'paper-mills', 'document-factories' and 'talk-shops' as such documents, research and codes are considered in the eyes of the offended as useless. It follows then that disbursement for them is seen, at best, as a waste of money and inefficient and, at worst, corrupt.

Following this logic it comes then as no surprise that the current attacks on the organizations concentrate particularly on inefficiency and corruption and are notably lacking in pin-pointing, over a broad range, the substantive objections to the organizations' output. These charges come at a time when, as a result of the emergence of anti-hegemonic policies, the personnel of the international organizations have changed. More persons from the third world are now found in the position of executive-heads of the organizations and more persons from the third world are within the bureaucracies. A cynic from the third world might be excused for noting that the larger the number of executive heads and other personnel from the third world, the shriller the cries of corruption, inefficiency and nepotism arising from the major States of the first world. Such a cynic would be mistaken, however, for precisely the vitriolic language used against Mr M'Bow, the African executive head of UNESCO, was also used against one of his predecessors, the European Mr Maheu. Thus the charge made in 1985 that UNESCO under M'Bow was characterized by 'autocratic leadership, gross cronyism, the explicit abandonment of impartiality and questionable financial practices'[13] is not so different as that made in 1970 against UNESCO under Mr Maheu which was that the organization 'was choking on red tape and burying itself in paper – direction is virtually non-existant, usually arbitrary, sometimes absent and frequently misguided... the Director-General is invited to display a spirit of courtesy and consideration.'[14] Similarly with FAO – one author states in 1981 that 'FAO under Saouma [from Lebanon] is totally one-sidedly oriented' and staff feel that top people are not 'even capable of running a parking lot'.[15] Yet in 1976 'FAO funds are destined to pay [under Mr Boerma from The Netherlands] for a gigantic centralized bureaucracy in Rome, 11 per cent to put out publications that no one reads and the remaining 9 per cent to hold meetings and for travel expenses that are largely unnecessary',[16] according to Mr Saouma when he became executive head of the organization. In 1956 after a staff suicide in FAO there was reported a 'low morale' in the organization yet in 1981 it is reported that there is widespread stress with a high degree of alcoholism and absenteeism.[17]

The conclusion is that the problems identified now have always been there and criticisms based on them have been voiced before but at the time they were first made they were not used as an excuse to attack the whole organization, its work and its place in the world, nor did they provoke major States to leave the organizations entirely. The reason, of course, is that at that time the organizations were not pursuing anti-hegemonic policies. Now that the organizations do have such policies these factors of international bureaucracy are used as an excuse to undermine the whole work and existence of the organizations. In short, to silence the even weak international voices which are questioning the veracity, justice and viability of current world structures and practices.

It is clear that new orders, codes of conduct and their supporting publications tend to be anti-hegemonic, and tend therefore, in some way to shake the edifice of power and structure which in the current period so many administrations are more clearly committed to uphold and support; FAO in promoting agricultural self-sufficiency in the third world challenges the structure of international agriculture and the continued ability of food exporters to use 'food power'; WHO has continual skirmishes with the health-polluting industries and their supporting headquarter States; UNESCO battles with international press monopolies and the ILO starts to reveal the less tasteful aspects of the exploitation of the weakest sectors of the world labour force. It cannot but be expected that they will come under attack. What could be expected was that there would be more substantive analysis as to the real reasons why they come under attack and less facile acceptance of the vulgar headlines of inefficiency.[18] Only then can the real and needed reforms be disentangled from the generalized and histrionic criticism, the sole purpose of which is either to destroy the organizations themselves or drastically curtail their capacity for any meaningful role other than that of being lifeless instruments of the *status quo* and of real politic State craft.

The title of this chapter raises the question of international co-operation as a successor to functionalist intervention. The reason for the question mark behind 'international co-operation' in the title is the paucity of current hope that a more equal and meaningful international co-operation will emerge.

The activities of the UN agencies gather people together in a spirit of exchange and equality since the monopoly of expertise has ceased to be that of the ex-colonial powers. Both the officers of agencies of governments and non-governmental organizations are experiencing and learning bitter lessons from the actions and statements of the opponents of the tenets of the civil society, namely those of questioning the conventional wisdom, investigation and the presentation of truth as it is seen. The multiplication of solidarity groups and of international contacts surrounding specific issues in which the work of the UN social activity agencies are at the centre indicates a process of the deepening of international concern and consciousness about the misguided application of production management to social and professional concerns. Ironically there is a functionalist element involved – that of the international discourse between like-interested persons. How such a process and discourse gathers a momentum, how well the UN social activity agencies react to the challenges of the attacks made on them and how efficient their analysis of trends and strategies, will together determine whether the question mark inherent in international co-operation can be removed as progress is made towards a less hierarchic and more co-operative world.

Notes

The author is grateful for the comments of Nico Schrijver on an earlier draft of this chapter.

1) Figures from UN Joint Inspection Unit, *Some Reflections on Reform of the United Nations*, United Nations, Geneva, 1985.
2) Francis O. Wilcox, 'Importance of the UN Specialized Agencies to the UN', in: 14 *Department of State Bulletin*, March 19, 1956, pp. 480–486.
3) *Ibid.*, p. 480.
4) D. Mitrany, *A Working Peace System*, 1943, p. 42.
5) R.E. Riggs, 'The World Bank, the IMF and the WHO: More Data on Functionalist Learning' in: 24 *The Journal of Conflict Resolution*, 1980, p.350.
6) Francis O. Wilcox, *op. cit.* p. 486.
7) See *Report to the Government of Pakistan on Labour Conditions in Agriculture*, ILO, Geneva, 1955, as quoted in note 18 in J. Harrod, 'Ideology of the ILO Towards Developing Countries', in: *The Impact of International Organizations on Legal and Institutional Change in the Developing Countries*, International Legal Centre, New York, 1977, p. 48.

8) J. Harrod, 'Problems of the United Nations Specialized Agencies at the Quarter Century' in: 28 *The Year Book of World Affairs*, 1974, p. 196.

9) See S. Leonard, 'International Health and Transnational Business: Conflict or Co-operation?', in: 49 *Revue Internationale des Sciences Administratives* (3), 1983, pp. 259–68; K. Selvaggio, 'WHO Bottles up Alcohol Study: Why did the WHO Suddenly Drop Plans to Publish Study of World Liquor Industry – Alcohol Beverages – Dimensions of Corporate Power', in: 4 *Multinational Monitor* (9), 1983.

10) To take but two examples, UN Centre on Transnational Corporations: *Transnational Corporations in the Agricultural Machinery and Equipment Industry*, United Nations, New York, 1983; P. Phongpaichit, *From Peasant Girl to Bankok Masseuse*, ILO, Geneva, 1981.

11) See Leonard, *op. cit.* p. 262.

12) See Philippe Laurent, 'Vers un Nouvel Ordre Économique International: Dix Ans de Recherches', in: 358 *Etudes* (3), June 1983, pp. 755–68; for an article which outlines the transformation from an old order to new order incorporating the anti-hegemonic policies see M.C. Smouts, 'Crise des Organizations Internationales', in: 358 *Etudes* (2), February 1983, pp. 165–173; for a writer currently sympathetic to the changes in function of international organizations see Evan Luard, 'Functionalism Revisited: The UN Family in the Eighties', in: 59 *International Affairs*, 1983, pp. 649–692.

13) J. Ruggie quoting the *Wall Street Journal* and personal interviews in John Gerard Ruggie, 'United States and the United Nations: Towards a New Realism', in: 39 *International Organization* (2), 1985, p.33.

14) 'UNESCO Director Endorsed as Staff Unit Cites "Malaise" ', in: *International Herald Tribune*, June 19, 1970, p. 4; N.A. Sims reviewing Richard Hoggart, *An Idea and Its Servants: UNESCO from Within*, Chatto and Windus, London, 1978, notes that Hoggart, who worked as an Assistant Director-General for 5 years, saw Maheu as 'a kind of a monstre sacré, a bullying tyrant partially redeemed by his devotion to the Organization...' N.A. Sims, 'Servants of an Ideal: Hoggart's UNESCO and the Problem of International Loyalty', in: 11 *Millennium: Journal of International Studies* (1), 1982, p. 65.

15) O. Matzke, 'Insufficient Control of Efficiency and Development Impact in the UN System: The Example of the FAO', in: 14 *Verfassung und Recht in Ubersee*, 1981, pp. 115–138.

16) *New York Times*, April 25, 1976.

17) *New York Times*, August 25, 1956, p. 16, and Matzke, *op. cit.* p. 135. For a study which finds the complete opposite to the 'inefficiency and corruption' found by Matzke see Chike P. Ilomechina, *Personnel Management and Industrial Relations in a United Nations Agency: History, Basis and Practice in the Food and Agricultural Organization*, Vantage Press, New York, 1983. Both authors, however, fail to acknowledge the

relative openness of the information about the organization and therefore the possibility that the same events and malpractices exist in large 'closed' organizations such as multinational corporations and government agencies.

18) This criticism can be levelled at the so-called 'Bertrand Report' – *Some Reflections on Reform of the United Nations* – prepared by Maurice Bertrand, United Nations, Geneva, 1985, which tends to ignore the source of criticisms, the power structure in which the organizations function, the bulk of the established literature on international secretariats and shows little interest in the concept of international public service.

Index

national power, widespread resistence
to supranational authority 30
nationalism 23, 136
New International Economic Order
12, 22, 47, 102
anti-hegemonic publications and
research 140
opposition to in WHO 139–40
tend to be anti-hegemonic 141
Nicaragua Case: *Military and
Para-military Activities in and
against Nicaragua (Nicaragua vs
the United States, 1986)* 49
non-governmental organizations
(NGOs) 20, 38, 125,136
importance of in functionalist thesis
135
law-making activities 38
non-intervention, duty of 43
non-reciprocity principle, erosion of 80
non-tariff barriers 76, 78
North Atlantic Treaty Organization
(NATO) 19
North Sea Continental Shelf cases
(1969) 48
North-South dialogue xii
noting patterns, change in 21-2, 24
nuclear arms race 11,15
poor performance of the UN 9
*Nuclear Test Cases (Australia and
New Zealand vs France, 1974)* 49

oil crises, and balance of payments
problems, role of IMF 61
oil-exporting countries 99
operational programmes, rise in 21
opinio juris 43
overemployment 118

para-medical personnel 138–9
peace economy, conversion to 14
peace-keeping forces 41
peace-keeping, development of 4

Permanent Sovereignty over Natural
Resources, Declaration on (1962)
45
permissive resolutions 45–6
plural society 119
pluralism 136
politicization 25
avoidance of 64, 65
development of in UNESCO 126–7
Poverty and Hunger, World Bank
Publication 109
poverty and hunger, Asian efforts to
alleviate 105
poverty, and development 100
poverty, hunger and malnutrition 96–7
primary health care, held back, refusal
to train para-medical personnel
139
primary products, as exports 77
private sector, participation in UN
decision-making process 20–1
professional discourse, globalization
of 137
programmatory resolutions 46–7
'progressive development' of
international law 34
prolongation, natural,
principle of 48
protectionism 62, 75, 78, 88
discussed by UNCTAD 85
hidden forms of 115–16
pseudo-economic concepts 80
purchasing power, lack of 97

reactive defense, third world 138
realist perspective in international
relations, supporting specialized
agencies 133
recession 85, 87
reciprocity 72–3, 78, 102
recommendations, and international
law 39
Red Cross, International Committee
(ICRC) 38